The Abortion Debate: TCU Voices

# The Abortion Debate: TCU Voices

Edited by

Charles K. Bellinger

Fort Worth, Texas | Churchyard Books | 2012

The Abortion Debate: TCU Voices

Printed by: www.createspace.com
Distributed by: www.amazon.com

Cataloging-in-Publication data:

Bellinger, Charles K., 1962-

    The abortion debate: TCU voices / edited by Charles K.
Bellinger.

    viii + 105 p.; 23 cm.

    ISBN-10: 1469904004
    ISBN-13: 978-1469904009

    1. Abortion—Moral and ethical aspects. 2.
Abortion—Religious aspects—Christianity. I. Title.

HQ767.15 .B48 2012

# Contents

EDITOR'S PREFACE

This book consists of a collection of essays written by students who have engaged the issue of abortion in courses that I have taught at Texas Christian University and Brite Divinity School from 2009-2011. For TCU, I taught a summer course entitled "The Abortion Debate" within the Master of Liberal Arts (MLA) program. For Brite, I taught a course entitled "Religion and Violence," which had a major section on the topic of abortion.

While the opinions of the students in the courses varied widely, reflecting the diversity of opinion within American society in general, my principle of selection was not ideological balance, but rather quality. I choose to include papers written by students who had consistently turned in the best quality work during the course as a whole, and on their abortion paper in particular. With that criterion, I decided to "let the chips fall where they may" in terms of the pro-choice to pro-life spectrum. As it turns out, the scale tips more to the pro-life side in this collection, which could perhaps reflect the relatively conservative cultural environment in Texas. I, the instructor, fall on the pro-life side of the debate, as is clear in my own contribution to the volume, but I deliberately taught the courses in such a way that my views were not a shaping force on student opinions. Some of the students may even have said after concluding the course that they were unsure what my views were.

The arrangement of the chapters is chronological. Deanna Darr, a school teacher, and Bonnie McClory, a nurse, took the MLA course in 2009. Jonathan Perry, a film critic and history grad student, and Heather Luensmann, an administrative assistant at TCU, took the MLA course in 2010. I presented my paper at a Colloquium on Violence and Religion conference in 2010. It was influenced by my study of Kenneth Burke in the English department at TCU. Walter Braddock, Jayme Harvey, Joshua Hurd, Rashona Thomas, and Justin Tiemeyer are all seminary students who wrote their papers in 2011. Stacey Solomon, who intends to go to law school, and Marcia Davis-

Seale, a journalist, took the MLA course in 2011. I included an op-ed piece she wrote for her newspaper after the course, rather than her final paper. All of the students enthusiastically agreed to have their thoughts published in this collection when I proposed that possibility to them.

Charles K. Bellinger
January, 2012

CHAPTER ONE

Aspects of the Pro-Life Movement

by Deanna Darr

The abortion debate has been going on for centuries. From ancient times, unwanted pregnancies have been terminated by various means, and the debate concerning whether abortion is right or wrong still ensues today during the 21$^{st}$ Century. The question of the rightness or wrongness of abortion is a settled question for the Pro-Life Movement, however. Whether they actually fight for the law allowing abortion to be repealed or not, pro-lifers object to abortion itself as murder, the ending of a life, with great zeal. There are many arguments that are put forth in this debate, consisting of religious, medical, life-trajectory, feministic, and educational, but all aspects have one thing in common—the sacredness of human life, especially that of the unborn child.

**Religious Aspects**
Many pro-life supporters base their arguments in religion. While Buddhists, Hindus, Jews, Muslims, Shinto practitioners, and other peoples have opinions about abortion in conjunction to their religion, the focus here is on Christianity and the main source of Scripture for that religion, the Bible. Christians argue that the fetus is a life based on the words of King David:

> For You formed my inward parts; You covered me in my mother's womb. I will praise You, for I am fearfully and wonderfully made; Marvelous are your works, and that my soul knows very well. My frame was not hidden from you, when I was made in secret, and skillfully wrought in the lowest parts of the earth. Your eyes saw my substance, being yet unformed, and in Your book they all were written, the days fashioned for me, when as yet

1

there were none of them. How precious also are Your thoughts to me, O God! (Psalm 139: 13-17 NIV)

From the moment of conception and throughout the intricate forming of the embryo, fetus, and eventually infant in the mother's womb, God was there and was making and planning this life. According to the Christian Bible, life begins from the moment of conception. From that moment, God creates a plan for the life of that baby, as referenced in Jeremiah 29:11: "'For I know the plans I have for you,' says the Lord, 'Plans to give you peace and not of evil, to give you a future and a hope.'" God's purpose is to give a future to each person's life, and abortion halts God's purpose. Pro-choice advocates argue that the future of the mother's life is the one that God is talking about here, but the pro-lifers will counter-argue that he is talking about *each* and *every* life, because he "came to give you life, and to give it more abundantly" (John 10:10).

Commands given in the Bible by God also show that abortion is not right and is not in God's plan. For instance, He makes many references to sex. Sex was created by God to be enjoyed and to cause procreation between a man and a woman who are husband and wife: "Marriage should be honored by all, and the marriage bed kept pure, for God will judge the adulterer and all the sexually immoral" (Hebrews 13:4). To stray from this covenant is to invite heartache and hardship. Fornication (sex before marriage), adultery (sex outside of marriage), rape, incest, and other sexual deviancies are strictly abhorred in Scripture. "The body is not meant for sexual immorality, but for the Lord, and the Lord for the body" (II Corinthians 6:13). The body that we souls inhabit does not belong to us—although the pro-choice movement will argue that a woman's body is her own to do with what she wishes—but to the Lord. "Do you not know that your body is a temple of the Holy Spirit, who is in you, whom you have received from God? You are not your own; you were bought as a price. Therefore honor God with your body" (II Corinthians 6:18-20). To stray from this belief is to stray from the commands of the Lord because "it is God's will that you should be holy: that you should avoid sexual immorality (I Thessalonians 4:3)," and giving in to temptation of sexual immorality can cause unwanted things to happen—things you will have to deal with because of your choice to have sex. Just as Adam and Eve had to live with the consequences of their choice in the Garden of Eden, which affected the entirety of humanity, so must each of us deal with our choices, and in this case, the choice to have sex.

Another command that is set forth in the Bible which is quoted against abortion is "Thou shalt not murder." If indeed the fetus is a life, then to terminate that life is to commit murder. Since this is one of the Ten Commandments, it must be a pretty important one because it affects not only the person murdered, but the murderer himself, the community, society, and the world as a whole. From the Christian Pro-Life perspective, abortion is akin to murder and therefore should not be done . . . ever.

## Medical Aspects

Even if one is not a Christian, or even not religious or spiritual, there is another aspect our society that agrees that the fetus is a life—the medical world. As recently as one hundred years ago, science had very little knowledge about conception, implantation, and pregnancy, but as medical and technological advancements have been made, the amount of knowledge has increased dramatically. Nowadays, we not only know the physical aspects of this process, we can watch it and take pictures of it through various medical tools.

Bernard Nathanson, author of *The Hand of God: A Journey from Death to Life by the Abortion Doctor Who Changed His Mind*, states: "it is said that if we grew at the same rate during our entire gestation as we do in the first two weeks of life, we would each weigh twenty-eight thousands pounds at birth" (4). These physiological changes and growth rates are happening to a life that began with the joining of two gametes (each with half the number of chromosomes that make up a human cell), the sperm and the egg. Alone, each of these has only half of what is needed to make a human life, but once joined, a completely different set of genes from that of the egg alone or the sperm alone is present, and a living cell is formed. This cell begins multiplying, creating the zygote. "Tiny hairlike cilia lining the fallopian tube propel the fertilized egg (zygote) through the tube toward the uterus. The cells of the zygote divide repeatedly as the zygote moves down the fallopian tube. The zygote enters the uterus in 3 to 5 days. In the uterus, the cells continue to divide, becoming a hollow ball of cells called a blastocyst"(www.Merck.com). This creature implants itself onto the wall of the uterus and continues dividing. As the cells are diving and differentiating, after only 6 weeks, the heartbeat of the new life is 140 to 150 beats per minute—around twice that of the mother carrying it! Non-living creatures do not have heartbeats. "The next stage in development is the embryo, which develops under the lining of the uterus on one side. This stage is characterized by the formation of most internal organs and external body structures. Organ formation begins about 3 weeks after fertilization, when the embryo elongates, first suggesting a human shape"(Merck). A *human* shape, not the shape of a plant or a fungus or another type of animal. It's the size of a pea, but not the shape of a pea. It's the size of a hazelnut, but not the shape of a hazelnut. When it reaches the size of a flying squirrel, it is not in the shape of a flying squirrel. It is in the shape of a human, and because of its genetic code and structure, it *is* a human. All of its human organs are formed by the 8th week of pregnancy, and from that point on, it's just a matter of growth. By 12 weeks of pregnancy, the fetus fills the entire uterus. By about 14 weeks, the sex of the fetus can be identified. By 16 to 20 weeks, the mother can feel the fetus moving, and by 24 weeks, there is a chance of survival outside of the uterus. This creature is alive, and it is human.

An intricate part of the medical aspect of pregnancy, birth, and abortion, is the doctor. When a person becomes a doctor, there is a standard code of ethics that he or she must subscribe to called the Hippocratic Oath, which traditionally stated: "I will give no deadly medicine to anyone if asked, nor suggest any such counsel; and in like manner, I will not give to a woman a pessary to produce an abortion." Bernard Nathanson, renowned abortion doctor turned pro-life activist, describes in detail his violation of this oath that he took when he aborted a child he had conceived with a woman. He scrubbed up and "put the Auvard speculum in the vagina after prepping the area with antiseptic solution . . . grasped the cervix with two tenacula, infiltrated a solution of pitressin . . . sounded the uterus . . . then dilated the cervix with the graduated shiny steel dilators. I placed the hollow plastic cannula into the uterus . . . when the gauge hit fifty-five millimeters of negative pressure I began sweeping the cannula around the interior of the uterus, watching the shards of tissue streaming through the hollow, translucent cannula on their way to the gauze trap . . . ." (Nathanson, *The Hand of God*, 59). This suction method that he used to abort the fetus is only one way to perform an abortion. Emmenagogues, drugs used to start the menstrual period, were used in the 18th and 19th centuries. Chemical poisons such as Methotrexate, came about in the 20th century, and in the 1980's, the RU-486 drug was invented and used. All of these medicinal abortive processes, as well as other surgical ones like a D&E (dilation and evacuation) resulted in the same thing as the suction method–the death and destruction of the fetus. In our time, the Hippocratic Oath has been edited, removing its prohibition of abortion.

**A Feministic Aspect**
In the case of an abortion, the pro-life view takes the side of the fetus nine times out of ten. But there are two parties involved in the decision (three if you count the father), and the second party is already a living, independent member of society–the mother. In order to see the entire spectrum of the abortion debate, the mother must not be ignored. Her choice of what to do with her body, because ultimately her vagina, cervix, and uterus belong to her, even if the fetus doesn't, is the issue of the debate. To ignore the mother is to ignore a vital part of the scenario, and focus must be given to her if there is ever any hope of changing her mind away from abortion. This is something that most pro-lifers don't understand, and this is why the pro-life movement is at a halt.

A woman who is facing an unwanted pregnancy often feels like her true self will be denied because of what is happening inside her body. By being pregnant, she is violating her own wants and desires, her own need for survival, and her own pleasure and/or advancement. Careers come to a halt, physical changes occur, and plans for a different future than what was originally conceived result because of conception. Having another being inside of her makes her feel like her self-identity is being eradicated. The pro-life movement's focus on the fetus does not hold any sway for her because she is concerned with herself. This may sound selfish, but it is actually what most people in society do when faced with any decision, so she cannot be faulted for it. Many of these women agree that abortion is murder, wrong and evil, but they believe that they truly have no choice, which is why they fight for the choice to have an abortion. According to Paul Swope, "Her central, perhaps subconscious, question is rather, 'How can I preserve my own life?' The pro-life movement must address her side of the equation, and do so in a compassionate manner that affirms her own inner convictions" ("Abortion: A Failure to Communicate," 33). Swope is an advocate of The Caring Foundation, a group that represents the pro-life movement to the public via television. Their aim is to educate women about the possibilities afforded them besides abortion, but they do so by putting the woman first so that she feels more at ease making a decision against abortion, one that will ultimately help her in the end. Women, especially women who are faced with this decision, need to be presented with believable role models that are not condemning to them but are supportive of them. A focus should be made on the woman in the situation, not just on the fetus. No one has all the answers, but helping women build their self-esteem, establish their own identity within a pregnancy, and enhance their beliefs that they can handle this circumstance without resorting to abortion, helps find the answers. Swope ends his article with the statement: "The terrible miscalculation of young women is that abortion can make them 'un-pregnant,' that it will restore them to who they were before their crisis. But a woman is never the same once she is pregnant, whether the child is kept, adopted, or killed. Abortion may be a kind of resolution, but it is not the one the woman most deeply longs for, nor will it even preserve her sense of self. If those of us in the pro-life movement can help women see this for themselves, we will have done much to disengage our culture from the abortion mentality"(35).

## Alternatives to Abortion
Abortion is not the only alternative measure that can be used or done when faced with an unwanted pregnancy. Keeping the baby or putting it up for adoption are also choices, as the pro-life side will undoubtedly argue; and it is a part of the choice, which the pro-choice side usually ignores. Of course, no choice is the perfect one, because even the two choices that result in giving the baby life have their drawbacks. If one agrees with religion and medicine, however, that the fetus is a life, and if one concedes that the trajectory of any life can be impactful to our world, and if one believes that the woman is a valuable part of the equation, one must also agree that the other two options are the better alternatives.

Keeping the baby is a difficult choice. If it was an easy one, abortion would never have been an option in the first place. A woman who is poor, uneducated, unsupported, or even worse, raped or a victim of incest must have the encouragement, help, and assistance that she needs in order to make this choice. Telling a woman that she must choose to keep the baby, then allowing her to attempt this with no aid or fostering of care is a crime in and of itself. It is ignoring the problem that led to the contemplation of abortion in the first place. This is where the pro-life movement comes in. One major way to help these women is through a Crisis Pregnancy Center.

The Mid-Cities Crisis Pregnancy Center in North Richland Hills, Texas is a prime example of a place where women with an unplanned pregnancy may go to get information not only on abortion, but also on other alternatives as well as pre- and post-natal care. The services there are free—to accommodate the poor and uneducated—and confidential—to accommodate the unsupported and frightened. At the center, they begin with a free pregnancy test, then they educate the woman about the first nine months of a child's life, beginning with conception and following through until birth. They have a special section of counseling for women who have had abortions and are dealing with PAS (Post-Abortion Syndrome), which is a version of Post-traumatic Stress Disorder. They list the symptoms of physical, behavioral, emotional, and relationship problems that can result because of this disorder, and they have an 8-week program that helps a woman deal with the results of an abortion. There is even a portion of their center that is dedicated to the men and helps them deal with the fact that they are now the father of a baby, whether the choice the mother makes is abortion, adoption, or keeping the baby.

At the Mid-Cities pregnancy center, all options are explored with the woman before she makes her decision. Abortion is not ignored as a possibility, even though the center is pro-life, Christian-run, and abortion is not encouraged or performed there. The center lives in reality, though, and knows that ignoring this as an option means that the woman will get fewer options in the long run since abortion clinics often dismiss the possibilities of keeping the baby or putting it up for adoption. They provide information about abortion procedures and what the woman might face afterwards. As for the adoption option, they provide information and referrals to adoption centers as well as classes that inform the mother and help her through the process in case this is the way she chooses to go. Lastly, they provide information about parenting so that if the mother chooses to keep the baby, she is not left high and dry without any support or encouragement. The mother can take free classes in parenting, and the center donates maternity and baby clothes for the family. In fact, they even will talk to the fathers, parents, or other family members upon request in order to help make the transition easier on the mother.

In all, places like the Mid-Cities Pregnancy Center are essential to the pro-life movement if the true aim is to decrease the number of abortions. Opportunities like this alleviate the need for abortion because the woman who has an unwanted pregnancy can find information in the areas where she is uneducated, support if she is alone in this situation, and care if she chooses to go another route besides abortion. Having these things in place and available to these mothers eradicates their reasoning for having the abortion: I'm all alone, no one will stand by me in my pregnancy, I can't function as a mother, I am scared to give a baby up for adoption. All of these fears can be taken away by these kinds of centers.

**Giving Lives a Chance**
Have you ever played the game Six Degrees of Separation? The concept behind the game is that everyone in the world is connected by the people that they know. It's no secret that our lives are impacted by those around us, but have you ever thought of what your life would have been like had you not been in the place you are? One of the most famous Christmas movies in the world, *It's a Wonderful Life*, is about precisely that. George Bailey, with the help of an angel, is able to see into another world and experience how horrible life would have been for everyone he knew if he had never been born. "In the right place at the right time" incidents happen every day, and while they could be chalked up to mere coincidence, they are nonetheless real experiences. It is also no secret that had certain people not been born, things in the world would have been different. For instance, if Hitler had not been born, WWII may never have happened, and if Dwight Eisenhower had not been born, WWII may never have ended. If Jesus, Mohammed, and Buddha had not been born, our world would be vastly different religiously, and thus historically and philosophically, than it is today. If one thinks along those lines, one must also think about how the world could have been impacted had certain people never been aborted. Even pro-choicers cannot argue against the fact that a fetus is a possible life, even if they argue against religion and science/medicine that it is already a life. If allowed to live, the fetus would have eventually been a baby, a toddler, a child, a

teenager, and an adult, and who knows what kind of things he or she would have done!

Many famous people were nearly or could have been aborted and were not, and thus our world is the way it is today because of them. One argument of the pro-choice side is that abortion-on-demand allows for mothers to choose whether or not to have their babies if there is a defect in the fetus, thus saving the fetus from a life of handicaps and the mother from the burden of caring for a child with a handicap. U.S. Representative Thaddeus Stevens (1792-1868), who helped draft the 14th Amendment and the Reconstruction Act, and Kristi Yamaguchi, the 1992 Olympic champion figure skater, were both born with clubfeet. John Wesley, one of the greatest evangelists of the 18th century, was born to a family that already had 14 children and was living in poverty in a world that was already at that time becoming vastly overpopulated. If John Wesley had not been born, many people would not have converted to Christianity, and the Methodist Church would likely never have come into existence. Ludwig van Beethoven was born the fifth child to a mother with TB and a father with syphilis, whose siblings included a blind child, a deaf child, a deceased child, and another with TB. Had Beethoven been aborted, which would have been the advice given to his mother when her circumstances were reviewed at an abortion clinic, the world of music would be vastly different than it is today. One day, a 13-year-old black girl was raped. This girl got pregnant from the rape, decided against having an abortion, and Ethel Waters, the famous and influential gospel singer, was born. And, most influential in the world, a teenage girl is pregnant and her fiancé is not the father. The result? Jesus Christ. Even if a person does not believe that Jesus is the Son of God, nor do they worship Him, every historian will agree that He was one of the most influential people ever to live. Our society and the entire world would be completely different had Mary gotten an abortion.

Heisman Trophy winner Tim Tebow, who quarterbacked for Florida, has an amazing "gosh I'm glad he wasn't aborted" story. Tebow is a very strong Christian, and he is known as a great inspirational speaker, and, according to his teammates, an amazing leader. In 1985, his parents lived in the Philippines, and his mother fell into a coma because of amoebic dysentery. They were able to save her, and she found out during the course of treatment that she was pregnant. The medication given to her to treat the disease were harmful to the fetus, and placental abruption occurred. The chances of the fetus surviving were small, and the doctor suggested abortion. Since this was years after the *Roe v. Wade* case, abortion was completely legal, and by this time relatively safe to the mother. Tebow's parents decided to take a chance and let their son be born, and besides being a little bit skinny and slightly malnourished at birth, he ended up being very healthy. So healthy, in fact, that he went on to play high school and college football, and won the Heisman trophy.

Famous people aside, what about the regular lay people who could have been aborted? Take, for instance, an influential teacher in a Title I school smack-dab in the middle of the slums, teaching children who come from poverty and sickness and dysfunction. This teacher tells her students each day that she loves them, and she means it, and that is a message they very rarely hear. This teacher takes each child individually and meets them where they are, patiently teaching them to read, to do math, to learn history, to perform science experiments. This teacher shows them the right way to behave in society in order to advance in this world. And the students of this teacher go on to break out of the trap of poverty, attend college or trade school because their teacher told them they were capable of doing it and they believed her; they may become influential politicians and doctors and lawyers and medical assistants and mechanics and architects and HVAC technicians and cosmetologists and anything else they want to be. This teacher was born in 1975, two years after abortion became legal, to a young woman who had no parental support and no job, whose best course of action, seemingly, would have been to abort. She had the child and gave her up for adoption. What about that regular person who changes the world just by existing?

Several years ago, a 19-year old mother found herself pregnant in Houston, Texas from a one-night stand. She had a thriving acting and modeling career and was planning to move to L.A. to pursue more in the performing arts as soon as she had enough money. Her parents were ex-pats in Indonesia, and she was living alone in the big city with no one to turn to. She had enough money to get an abortion, and she had the legal right to get an abortion since abortion had been legalized a few years before. Instead, she went to the Catholic Diocese of Houston and lived there in their crisis pregnancy unit, right next door to the hospital. She had chosen to have the baby and give it up for adoption, and she went through the process and was taken good care of until the time for birth came—which was early. Because she had bonded with the baby while carrying it in her womb, she refused to leave the premature infant alone until she knew that the baby would be okay. A few weeks later, the baby reached 5 pounds and was taken out of the incubator, off the ventilator, and was given to a new set of parents. The woman went on with her life and her career, never forgetting about the baby, and never regretting that she didn't have an abortion and chose adoption instead. Twenty-six years later, via the internet, the woman and the child (now a grown-up) found each other, and she was reassured that she did the right thing. The baby grew up in a loving home, was given the best of everything, and had received an amazing education and an amazing family. She was showered with love and attention and never regretted for a moment that she was not aborted and was instead given up for adoption. This paragraph and the previous one are describing the same situation, which is a true story. I am that baby, that "fetus."

CHAPTER TWO

Products of Conception

by Bonnie L. McClory

It came as a profound shock to me when a tiny girl who never drew breath taught me an important lesson about life. She would have been thirty-eight years old now, had her embarrassed grandparents not found an unscrupulous hypocrite of a doctor to end her life. I do not know if the young woman who bore her ever thinks of her, but I do. I do, because my arms were the only ones that ever cradled her lifeless body; my tears were her baptismal waters. The wrongness of her death became a powerful force in my life. Because of her, some who might have shared her fate now live.

Let me begin at the beginning. (I started my career in women's health as an obstetric technician in a large metropolitan hospital. OB techs, as they called us, were ancillary nursing personnel, specially trained by the hospital to assist the doctors and nurses in Labor and Delivery. We were supposed to be glorified nurses' aides. However, the hospital made a big mistake when they chose the women in my training class. We were all intelligent, college-educated women, hungry for knowledge and possessing the ability to use it. Our instructor, a wise and wonderful nurse, soon realized we were not a typical class. Instead of the twelve-week training course designed for OB techs, she taught us the obstetric curriculum for student nurses. We aced it, every single one of us.

My status in the class was that of the maverick. I was staunchly pro-life; my views arose from my own experience of being unintentionally pregnant at seventeen and a mother at eighteen. None of my classmates had ever borne a child; only one was married. I had already given birth to two sons and had seen my marriage disintegrate. My classmates did not seem too affected by our having to watch a first trimester abortion from the operating room gallery as part of our training. I sat among them, tears staining my white scrub dress; they chatted about the handsome resident doing the procedure and how lucky the teenage patient was to be able to get on with her life. I fought nausea as I watched that handsome resident piece together what he had removed from the teenager's uterus as he made sure he got it all out. My classmates turned away from the sight of the little mound of red flesh laid out in the small metal basin. They turned away from my obvious grief, as well.

Still, they were nice enough women and we got along well in general. I taught them the natural childbirth techniques I had learned for my own deliveries so they could help their laboring patients. They taught me that I was some kind of a throwback, as they attempted to gently change my mind about abortion. Sure, it was sad, but also necessary. Sisterhood is powerful! Our bodies, ourselves! Women have a right to be freed from unwanted pregnancy! It was all very 1970's feminist and it did nothing but make me wonder if I descended from a different species of human. Abortion bothered me.

Assisting at the actual abortion procedure was not part of our job. Back then, they were all done in the sanctum sanctorum, the operating room, whether they were the first trimester suction procedures done in the first thirteen weeks of pregnancy or the second trimester saline infusions, done up until twenty weeks. We occasionally had a first trimester post-operative patient in our recovery room on the weekends; the only contact I had with them was to take their vital signs and bring them ice chips. The patients who had saline abortions ended up in Labor and Delivery, though, because the procedure induced labor. We OB techs were supposed to provide the supportive care to these patients while they labored and assist the doctor when he or she delivered the dead fetus. None of my OB tech colleagues liked this part of the job. I heard them rationalize it, though, as a woman's right to choose. But it broke my heart, every time the doctor handed me a basin with a small perfectly-formed human baby lying dead and bloody inside it. I forced myself to rationalize that I had done nothing to bring about this death; I was merely cleaning up the aftereffects. That way, I could live with myself.

Labor and delivery was mostly a happy place to work. The hospital had the largest maternity service in the city, over four hundred births a month. We were always busy and I was always overworked, but I loved my job. Helping to bring new life into the world became not only my vocation, but my avocation. I read books on midwifery and obstetrics and took childbirth educator classes. I joined the local natural childbirth association and the fledgling homebirth movement. A scrapbook containing notes and baby pictures my patients sent me remains one of my prized possessions. In a few of those pictures, I am holding the newborn in the delivery room or helping the new mother to nurse. At last, I had found my niche. The only fly in the ointment was the abortion schedule.

Saline abortions became more and more frequent in the Labor and Delivery unit. In an effort to cope, I read about the procedure, hoping against hope that it was not as horrible as my mind imagined it to be. It wasn't – it was worse. The physician first raised a skin wheal with a local anesthetic on the maternal abdomen. Then a long needle was inserted into the uterus, through the numbed abdominal area. A fairly large amount of amniotic fluid was withdrawn from the uterus and then replaced with hypertonic saline. Hypertonic saline caused the fetal cells to burst. Death ensued shortly, but not before the fetus convulsed in death throes. Sometimes the mothers could feel these convulsions, depending on how far along in pregnancy they were.

The doctors usually attended the saline abortion deliveries, which could be complicated. Many of the fetuses were born feet first. Delivering the small head could be challenging because the opening of the uterus, the cervix, sometimes closed down around the head, trapping it. Once I saw a doctor pull so hard, he detached the body from the trapped head. Of course, the fetus was already dead, but he was as horrified as I was; I saw his eyes above his blue facemask. I guess it was a good thing they routinely kept the abortion patients heavily medicated. The few patients who refused sedation had varying responses to their abortion, but most became agitated, a few hysterical. Some asked the sex of the aborted fetus. All of them looked away from the towel-covered basin containing the dead baby.

My role was limited to opening sterile packs and cleaning up afterwards. Cleaning up meant boxing up the fetus in a round, white, one-gallon cardboard container – the kind you see in ice cream stores. I had to place one of the mother's identification stickers on the box and then put it into the specimen refrigerator, awaiting its eventual destination in the pathology lab. At times I was the unwilling midwife, forced into delivering those poor lifeless mites when I was the one who walked into the labor room to find them half born. I still remember their dusky color, caused by the burst cells, and the smell, that smell that fills my memory as I write. The smell was not foul, but it was peculiar, and I could identify it to this day. I could also identify the gender of those fetuses; they were fully formed, even if they were only five to eight inches long. I hated this part of my job. The only way I could protest was to secretly conditionally baptize those fetuses whose mother's religious preference was a denomination of Christianity. If the mothers were not Christian, I said a simple prayer instead, committing the soul of the dead unborn to God.

One afternoon, my assignment was to care for a teenager who was laboring following a saline infusion. I remember looking at her chart, seeing the usual state-required physician certification that the pregnancy was less than twenty weeks – remember this was in the early 1970's – and noting when the doctor injected the saline, how long the patient had been laboring, and the time of her last Demerol injection. I carried the usual little birth kit into her labor room; we did not bother to open a standard delivery room for an abortion patient. Before I had time to introduce myself, much less take her vital signs, it was obvious she was about to deliver. I hit the call buzzer to summon help, opened the birth kit, donned my sterile gloves and proceeded to deliver a nearly four pound dead baby girl, about fifteen inches long, with a full head of hair. Though I tried to hide the little body from the patient, she saw it, and began screaming. "It's a baby! My baby! My baby!"

A doctor finally rushed in, looked about and curtly told me to take the specimen to the utility room, pronto. A nurse then showed up, a large syringe of potent narcotic in her hand, and quickly jabbed the patient. As the patient's screams subsided into loud, hiccupping sobs down the hallway, I stood in the utility room, my hands shaking as I attempted to box up the fetus, as I usually did. My eyes already knew what my mind would not accept: this fetus was too large for the one gallon specimen container. The usually no-nonsense head nurse poked her head into the room, saw the grisly situation, and told me in hushed tones to get a baby shroud and clean and dress the fetus for the morgue.

Baby shrouds were for infants born dead after twenty weeks. They were like loose white cotton nightgowns that tied in the front. The baby shroud pack contained a series of wraps and ties, designed to be placed just so, to avoid damage to the body during transport to the morgue. There were two small manila tags with short cheesecloth strings hanging from them, too. One was the baby's identification tag, meant to be tied loosely around the ankle. The other tag went on the outside of the neat cloth bundle I would make of the tiny body.

( She was beautiful, even in death. I gently cleaned her, patting her skin dry so it would not peel. Her silky fair hair had a slight curl to it after I washed it. She had long eyelashes, high cheekbones, and a tiny cleft in her chin. Her fingers were long and delicate, tiny nails dotting their ends. After I dressed her and tagged her, I conditionally baptized her. Her mother, I knew from the records, was Catholic. I held her in the crook of my left arm, against my heart – the same place I always held my own babies – and poured a few drops of water over her cool forehead. My tears mixed with the water as I baptized her. "If you are able to receive this sacrament, I baptize you in the name of the Father, the Son, and the Holy Spirit. Amen." Then I hugged her close in a great gasping sob and, in a gesture any mother would recognize, placed a kiss at the top of her little head. After I had done it, I realized it would be the only kiss she would ever receive. )

The outer cloth of the baby shroud covers the face. After I committed her face to memory, I finished with her death wrappings. She was a small white bundle now, but anyone could have guessed by the shape that it was a dead baby. Hospital protocol demanded that I put her little body into a rolling baby bassinet, the kind with a clear plastic box on top and metal legs below. I added some rolled baby blankets around her then covered her and the blankets with a couple of clean surgical towels, to look like I was transporting only blankets. Rolling this sad cortege past the nurses' station I picked up the necessary paperwork from the clerk and headed toward the back elevator. As I did so, I heard a woman asking the clerk if she could see her daughter. It was my patient's name she gave. I stopped and glanced back over my shoulder. A well-dressed couple in their mid-forties stood there. She had several diamond rings on her long, long fingers. He had fair, wavy hair and a cleft in his chin. Bile rose in my throat and it took every ounce of strength not to scream. The elevator came. I wheeled the little bassinet on board, pressed the button for the basement, and safely delivered her to the morgue. The young Jamaican attendant on duty gently lifted the small bundle from the bassinette as I signed the morgue's log book. "Ah, God's got himself another little angel," he said in his soft island lilt. "Yes, He has," I replied.

On returning to the Labor and Delivery floor, my head nurse pulled me into her office to see if I was okay. As her nickname was The Drill Sergeant, I was a little surprised at her sensitivity. I told her I was fine and asked to be reassigned. She told me she had already done that; I would be working "in the back" for the rest of my shift, setting up sterile delivery tables, taking inventory, stocking shelves, and ordering what we needed from Central Supply. It wasn't punishment. She was giving me a break because she knew I was rattled. I thanked her and turned to leave, then stopped in my tracks. My back to her, I said, "Nancy, how could that doctor mistake a nearly eight months baby for an eighteen weeker? Even I can tell the difference when I palpate a pregnant abdomen."

"Turn around, dear." I did so. Her eyes were damp, like she was going to cry. "He knew right well she was that far along. Her parents are friends of his. Don't say another word. It will all come out in the wash."

I knew she meant it would end up in the physicians' internal review committee, where doctors slapped each other on the wrist when they made mistakes that did not end up in litigation. I also knew the review committee was just a formality and that nothing would be done. Back then, we did not have ultrasound machines to determine fetal age; it all depended on the skill—or duplicity – of the obstetrician. At the end of my eight hours on duty, I submitted my resignation. I would never again become an unwilling accessory after the fact to murder.

After I left that hospital, I began working in quiet ways to assist women with crisis pregnancies. No big organizations or marches for me, as my new marriage and growing family required most of my time and energy. I simply let the word get out that I was willing to help. A friend's teenage daughter became part of my family as she brought the baby she would give up for adoption to term. A niece was born who almost wasn't. Granted, these were small victories, but they will always be infinitely precious to me.

Years later, I finally realized my dream of becoming a registered nurse. The only department in which I wanted to work was Labor and Delivery. By this time, out-patient clinics were doing most of the abortions. However, late abortions still were being performed in some Labor and Delivery units. Needless to say, I would not accept a job in those places, no matter how perfect everything else about the job was. When the hiring managers asked why I would not accept the positions they tendered, I was frank. I told them I would have nothing, absolutely nothing to do with terminating a baby's life. My stance cost me job advancement opportunities and angered some of my colleagues when they learned of my views. I have accepted whatever comes to me because of it. By refusing to participate in any part of the abortion procedure, I ceased to be a cog in a brutal machine. No, I am no martyr for my cause. That little bundle I took to the morgue all those years ago, she was the martyr.

CHAPTER THREE

Civil Obedience: A Pro-Life Defense of *Roe v. Wade*

by Jonathan Perry

A woman in the United States who chooses to abort a pregnancy in the early stages has the law on her side–for now.

In her 1996 book *Why I Am An Abortion Doctor*, Suzanne Poppema, one of the most outspoken and maddeningly dogmatic voices in the American pro-choice movement, wrote "I believe that the abortion issue can never regress to a point where it would be made illegal again" (Poppema, 233). But 14 years later, as the Tea Party movement gains electoral momentum and "pro-life" increasingly becomes a moniker synonymous with "religious right," politicians Democrat and Republican, liberal and conservative are faced with almost unbearable pressure to concede legal restrictions on the abortion rights guaranteed by 1973's *Roe v. Wade*.

Growing anti-abortion sentiment in the legislative arena might seem to be hopeful news for the pro-life movement–but for the pro-lifer of a more "gradualist" position (to borrow the terminology of Lisa Harris) than "no abortions, ever," it is anything but. Too often, the moral repugnance of voluntary pregnancy termination overshadows two greater concerns–the sanctity of the rule of law, and the health and safety of women. Reducing the rate of abortions in this country is achievable without compromising either, and in turn, placing the foundations of our society in peril.

**The Ruling**
Almost four decades have eclipsed and eight American presidents have sat in the Oval Office since the U.S. Supreme Court decreed abortion to be an individual right protected by our nation's Constitution. Yet the furor surrounding the *Roe v. Wade* decision, the court's most controversial ruling since the infamous

1857 *Dred Scott v. Sandford*, continues to accelerate–an ongoing invective fueled to a copious degree by misunderstanding and selective interpretation of the ruling's intent.

The cause of action for Norma McCorvey (aka "Jane Roe") against Dallas County District Attorney Henry Wade, as framed by plaintiff's attorneys Linda Coffee and Sarah Weddington, was not the explicit right to terminate a pregnancy, per se–but a woman's right to privacy. A horrific effect of this ruling has been a preponderance of abortions, to the tune of some 35 million within two decades, in the estimation of McCorvey (who worked in public relations and support roles for abortion clinics until her philosophical shift to a pro-life perspective in the mid-1990s) (McCorvey, 154). The high rate of abortions is particularly unfortunate because the *intent* of the decision in the plaintiff's favor was not to open the door to wholesale "abortion on demand" in rendering unconstitutional state laws that prohibited pregnancy termination for reasons other than rape or endangerment to a mother's life and health, but to affirm a constitutional right within the context of a regulated practice whose legality was granted–but whose exercise was not explicitly *encouraged*. The language of the *Roe v. Wade* ruling is deliberate in avoiding such an endorsement.

"Appellant and some *amici* (friends of the court) argue that the woman's right is absolute and that she is entitled to terminate her pregnancy at whatever time, in whatever way, and for whatever reasons she alone chooses. With this we do not agree," wrote Justice Harry Blackmun in his majority opinion. "The Court's decisions recognizing a right of privacy also acknowledge that some state regulation in areas protected by that right is appropriate. ... We, therefore, conclude that the right of personal privacy is included the abortion decision, but that this right in not unqualified and must be considered against important state interests in regulation" (Baird, 67).

Paramount among those "state interests," and the purported philosophical impetus behind the myriad state laws abolishing abortion from the late 19th century into the early 1970s, was the health and safety of a mother bearing a child–during an era when sepsis, uterine tears and other complications arising from abortion procedures accounted for a mortality rate among mothers that neared and perhaps even eclipsed that of childbirth. Laws prohibiting abortion were seen as a necessary reaction to a public health issue, and this argument bore significant heft until the prevalence of antibiotics in the 1940s to combat post-operative infections eliminated many of the common risks involved in pregnancy-termination procedures. Blackmun makes significant note of this in his *Roe v. Wade* opinion, noting that "modern medical techniques have altered this situation" (Baird, 65).

**"The Bad Old Days"**

Ironically, most of those modern medical techniques were developed during the era of wholesale abortion illegality–and practiced by licensed medical professionals in a clinical environment for the purposes of aborting a fetus, but legally only within the context of pregnancies that either endangered a mother's life or were a result of sexual assault (the latter of which, in the majority of states, had to be verified by a police report before an abortion exemption could be granted). But the fact remained that women continued to seek ways to terminate a pregnancy for a seemingly endless array of reasons–few of which were "legal."

The era of the "back-alley butcher" was born. In 1940, the U.S. Bureau of Vital Statistics reported 1,679 deaths in the U.S. as a result of botched abortions, performed illegally by shadowy figures armed with dubious or nonexistent medical credentials, preying upon scared women in desperate circumstances and demanding cash up front for the "service" of dismembering a fetus inside the womb with unsterilized instruments–often on a soiled kitchen table with not even a local anesthetic, as dramatized in Nancy Savoca's 1996 teleplay *If These Walls Could Talk*. These statistics do not include deaths, possibly numbering in the thousands annually, that were believed to be abortion-*related*: women who contracted hepatitis from infected blood following a transfusion to treat post-abortion hemorrhaging, for example; pelvic abscess caused by perforation of the uterus during a pregnancy termination; ectopic pregnancy caused by tubal pathology incurred during an illegal fetus extraction.

However, by 1967, the year the first U.S. state legalized abortion, the nationwide mortality rate from illegal abortions had dropped to 120. By 1977, that number had plummeted to a mere 21. As abortion became more available to women, the "back-alley butcher" saw his business nosedive– until *Roe v. Wade* sent him packing altogether.

Yet we should be loath to forget this dark chapter in American medical history–and memories are getting shorter as the 37ᵗʰ anniversary of the historic Supreme Court ruling approaches, warns Lisa Harris, a veteran abortion provider. "As the generation of doctors who provided abortions prior to *Roe v. Wade* retires," she writes, "the cadre of doctors who now provide abortions are no longer personal witnesses to the horrific sequelae of unsafe abortions" (Harris, 78).

Any number of circumstances can compel a frightened and desperate woman to terminate an unwanted pregnancy, and seldom on a "whim" or "caprice," as Justice Byron White wrote in his dissenting opinion on *Roe v. Wade*: unemployment, the stigma of unwed motherhood in conservative environments, lack of family support (emotional and financial), shame as the result of an extramarital affair, or simple terror at being faced with a life-changing situation. History has proven such women will find an avenue for abortion one way or another–and in the interests of public health, she must continue to be guaranteed the right to secure the necessary procedure under the auspices of licensed professionals in a safe, clinical environment. To deny her this right is not "pro-life," but "anti-choice."

**Parallel Lives**
We must recognize that right does not extend to late-term abortions, however–procedures in which the peril to a mother's health and safety (even in legal, clinically sanctioned circumstances) increases exponentially beyond first-trimester pregnancy terminations. Individual states do (and should) reserve the right to restrict abortions after the point of fetal viability, provided the laws contain the necessary loopholes accounting for rape, incest and endangerment to a mother's life if the pregnancy is carried to term.

The federal judiciary also is clear on this point. "... The State has legitimate interests from the outset of the pregnancy in protecting the health of the woman and the life of the fetus that may become a child," wrote Justices Sandra Day O'Connor, Anthony Kennedy and David Souter in the majority opinion of *Planned Parenthood v. Casey*, the 1992 ruling that upheld the *Roe v. Wade* decision. "These principles do not contradict each other; and we adhere to each" (Baird, 93).

Even pro-choice advocate Harris, while arguing for the necessity of second-trimester abortions in circumstances other than those described in *Planned Parenthood v. Casey*, acknowledges not only the "violence" of termination procedures performed during and beyond the second trimester, but that *two* lives are at stake past a certain point in pregnancy. A proponent of the "gradualist" position on abortion, Harris stops short of conceding a state interest in protection of the fetus that supersedes the rights of the mother, but her implication is clear that disputing the "personhood" of a fetus once pregnancy advances past the first trimester is a futile argument that is morally untenable, and is neither within the letter nor spirit of *Roe v. Wade*. "The respect owed to a fetus increases as pregnancy advances and the fetus becomes more like a born person," she writes. "There is no 'bright line' here—not even viability—that distinguishes what is morally acceptable or not, or prohibited or not. That is, even as we think that abortion is morally permissible, we are also permitted increasing discomfort, grief or loss with later abortions" (Harris, 79).

## A "Lincolnian" Approach

Harris' latter point is key, as it constitutes a concession by a prominent voice in the pro-choice movement that morality is a critical component of the abortion debate, and she hardly stands alone in this perspective. Feminist author Naomi Wolf, in her 1995 essay for *The New Republic* titled "Our Bodies, Our Souls," decried the propensity of the pro-choice movement to cede the language of "right and wrong" to opponents of abortion: "By refusing to look at abortion within a moral framework, we lose the millions of Americans who want to support abortion as a legal right but still need to condemn it as a moral iniquity" (Baird, 179). National Abortion and Reproductive Rights Action League (NARAL) chairman Kate Michelman told a *Philadelphia Inquirer* reporter in 1993 (in a statement she attempted to retract, but was recorded on audiotape), "We think abortion is a bad thing" (McKenna, 54). No less prominent a figure on the national stage than Secretary of State Hilary Rodham Clinton, speaking in the context of her husband's campaign for national health care reform in 1993 (a proposal that would have included federal funding for abortion), characterized voluntary pregnancy termination simply as "evil" (McKenna, 66).

So if even proponents of the pro-choice philosophy acknowledge abortion as "evil," why does the legally sanctioned practice of it continue? Because the rule of law, applied without passion or prejudice (to paraphrase Thomas Jefferson crudely), must prevail for the republic to prosper. The U.S. Supreme Court also speaks to this position, in the majority opinion for *Planned Parenthood v. Casey*. "Some of us as individuals find abortion offensive to our most basic principles of morality, but that cannot control our decision," Justices O'Connor, Kennedy and Souter write. "Our obligation is to define the liberty of all, not to mandate our own moral code" (Baird, 95).

In reconciling moral indignation with the best interests of the republic (and the individual's place within it), George McKenna draws a parallel between abortion and Abraham Lincoln's agonizing crisis over the issue of slavery. Lincoln, both during his rise to political prominence and during his tenure in office, placed preservation of the union above his personal repulsion at the institution of human bondage; his "gradualist" position, if you will, was not to call for the outright abolition of slavery but to "arrest the further spread of it, and place it where the public mind shall rest in the belief that it is in the course of ultimate extinction" (McKenna, 60). McKenna's perspective is distinctly pro-life, but hardly of the ilk of the absolutist positions that have hampered the pro-life perspective by assuming the "all or nothing" viewpoint regarding abortion–the "nuance is for wussies" philosophy that became *de rigeur* under the previous presidential administration.

By invoking Lincoln in *The Atlantic Monthly* essay "On Abortion: A Lincolnian Position," and employing commensurate rationale in equating abortion to white supremacist groups and other marginal sects society deems morally repugnant but must allow to operate within constitutional strictures, McKenna suggests a code of conduct for the conscientious objector who is morally repulsed by the prevalence of voluntary pregnancy termination but understands abortion cannot be rendered illegal across the board: "permit, restrict, discourage" (McKenna, 60). *Contain* the cancerous growth, as McKenna argues in summoning Lincoln, and accomplish this by widening the spectrum of choices available for a woman bearing an unwanted child: Adoption, single-parenthood counseling (which is subsidized in the majority of states), sanctuary homes not only for pregnancy terms but the first six months following childbirth via charitable organizations such as the Missouri-based Vitae Caring Foundation.

Incidentally, in producing a campaign of pro-life television commercials bearing the simple appeal for women to "Think About It," the Caring Foundation yielded a series of remarkable results beginning in the late 1980s: From 1988 to 1992 as the commercials aired in heavy rotation, the abortion rate in Missouri dropped 29 percent. In 1997, a 13-week TV campaign by the Foundation in the greater Boston area yielded a shift (according to polls conducted after the ads' airings) of 308,000 adults in the area who switched to a pro-life position after viewing the commercials. The Caring Foundation campaign is an exemplar of how positive steps toward reducing the abortion rate are possible without intrusive legislation.

To couch McKenna's argument on a more contemporary level, consider the Paula Jones-Monica Lewinsky scandal that consumed the latter years of Bill Clinton's presidency. The fatal miscalculation by Republicans seeking the president's ouster was to frame his transgressions as a *legal* matter–and not only did Clinton escape removal from office during his impeachment trial, but Americans rewarded "Slick Willie" with the highest approval ratings of his tenure in office. Reasonable citizens recognized Congress' dog-and-pony show as what it was, two successive Speakers of the House resigned in shame, and the level of confidence in our legislative branch has been sliding downward ever since. Yet, if lawmakers had foregone grasping at the straws of legality where none existed–and instead taken to the airwaves with a position of *moral* outrage removed from the pretense of law, Clinton's place in history most likely would have been irrevocably tainted.

A valuable lesson for the pro-life movement lies within the Clinton scandal: A favorable consensus can build quickly if the public perceives morality to be on your side, but society is apt to react violently if expected to embrace a dubious legality. Fight the good fight from the moral high ground the pro-choice camp has all but ceded to us, protest the evil of abortion in every forum possible within the confines of the law, cherish your personal liberty that allows you to do so–and ask yourself: If the constitutional right to privacy is restricted by a reversal of *Roe v. Wade*, what, ultimately, will you have won? The precedent set in scaling back one constitutional right with a judicial rebuke of *Roe v. Wade* could open the door for activist jurists to tamper with others–and in distant generations, in a different political climate, a judiciary armed with such a precedent just as easily could allow state laws *mandating* abortion for mothers who already have borne what a legislature might arbitrarily decide is "too many children." Such a line is simply too precarious to tread.

Beyond the right to privacy, another key constitutional issue is at hand in the *Roe* decision. In the Court's view, the unborn in the first trimester of pregnancy "at most, represents only the potentiality of life"(Baird, 69). However, myriad state abortion laws prior to the 1973 ruling and initiatives such as the Ronald Reagan administration's failed Human Life Amendment, which sought a federal ban on abortion, "openly linked public policy to the most traditional and conservative Roman Catholic theory on human fertility control" (Paul Simmons in Baird, 220) in defining "personhood" as beginning at the point of conception.

Such laws, which would become permissible in the event of a *Roe* reversal, would represent a tacit government endorsement of a specific religious doctrine–and, as such, a clear violation of the First Amendment's "establishment cause" prohibiting a "favored or official church of the nation" (Baird, 219). So says Paul Simmons of the University of Louisville, as he speaks sharply of the assault on religious freedom inherent in first-trimester anti-abortion laws, as does Roger A. Paynter, pastor of the First Baptist Church of Austin: "Since there is no moral consensus or biblical mandate, we should accord women the legal, moral, and religious freedom to choose" (Baird, 237).

**For Which It Stands**

Overruling *Roe v. Wade* could precipitate a constitutional crisis eclipsing even Richard Nixon's duplicity in covering up the Watergate burglary. As our democracy recovers from the Abu Ghraib scandal, the debacle of extralegal detentions at Guantanamo Bay, and myriad provisions of the U.S. Patriot Act that frequently teetered and occasionally face-planted along the slippery slope of constitutionality, I fear our republic could not withstand a blow as injurious as flouting five amendments in rejecting a ruling that has provided this nation with a perfectly serviceable blueprint of privacy rights for 37 years.

Ultimately, the decision whether to abort a pregnancy lies between the woman, her physician, and her God. The rule of law, as codified in *Roe v. Wade* and upheld in *Planned Parenthood v. Casey*, explicitly places the onus upon the individual states of the union to recognize and respect that compact that exists between those three aforementioned parties (again, within the strictures of the first trimester of pregnancy).

The federal *judiciary,* whose purpose is to interpret legislation in a manner that is consistent and inviolate of the U.S. Constitution, affirmed an individual woman's right to early-term abortion in *Roe v. Wade,* and further codified it in *Planned Parenthood v. Casey.* Like it or not, these rulings provide the blueprint of the "law of the land," as far as abortion is concerned. Positions on the abortion debate should not be, and never should have been, political currency for candidates of either party seeking election to a national office.

While removed from federal legislation, a sense of morality still plays an integral role in this process, so I'll espouse my own, borrowing the words of my late friend Karl Malden. Speaking on his unwavering friendship with Elia Kazan after the once-heralded filmmaker "named names" of presumed Communist sympathizers for the House Un-American Activities Committee, the elder statesman of stage and screen told me some 13 years ago, "*People* are more important than principles."

Those words have haunted me, and informed my modality of thinking as I have moved from the pro-choice beliefs of a liberal Presbyterian to rigidly pro-life, and back toward a more graduated pro-life perspective in my adulthood. The *people* at stake here are the mothers, the *principles* being a belief system that would mandate that a woman's health and welfare is superseded by the potentiality of the life she is carrying. The loss of tens of millions of *potential* lives to legal abortion is tragic almost beyond all comprehension–but an even greater tragedy would be to place even one *actual* life in peril because American women once again were forced to turn to unskilled, unscrupulous profiteers to end a pregnancy.

I personally find any abortion – at any stage of pregnancy – performed for reasons other than a violation of a woman's person through incest or sexual assault (and that stipulation *does* include spousal, date and statutory rape), or imminent danger to the mother's health, to be morally indefensible and an affront to decency. But abortion will continue to exist as long as sad, scared, desperate women, faced with unwanted pregnancy, believe they have no viable alternatives to denying the children in their wombs the right to life. As long as that reality remains, I will not–*cannot*–acquiesce to a philosophy that stipulates mothers should have to risk permanent injury at the hands of a charlatan with a dirty knife in the storeroom of a convenience store, or perhaps die, because their moral choice differs from mine.

CHAPTER FOUR

The Debate

by Heather Luensmann

It was a 7 to 2 majority vote on January 22, 1973. Some called it a giant leap for women's rights. Others deemed it a dark day in American history. To many it was a signal of freedom. To others it threatened the very sanctity of life. Regardless of political, moral, and social beliefs, it was a landmark decision.

When Justice Blackmun delivered the majority opinion in *Roe v. Wade*, it set into motion a tumult of events that are still debated today. On the face of the debate, it appears to be a simple one. But human life is never simple. Thus, abortion is not simple. It impacts the lives of women full of hopes and dreams. It impacts men directly and indirectly, and it impacts the silent, helpless fetus. So who will win the inevitable battle between woman and fetus? Perhaps it really is not a battle between the woman and the fetus but between the woman and the man or the woman and society.

The real issues of the abortion debate are much deeper than the surface issues of the timeliness of a pregnancy or the economic situation of a family. The debate is instead rooted deeply in the feminist movement and the life and subsequent rights of a fetus. Yet amidst this swirling atmosphere of questions and controversy, there remains a glimmer of hope through the options available to women facing the abortion decision.

But before looking at key topics within the abortion debate and the choices available to women, it would be appropriate to look at abortion as an industry. This can hopefully provide some perspective for later points.

## The Abortion Industry

Our society is fond of the reminder that insurance companies are in the business of making money. And, some believe that oil companies want to turn a profit at any environmental or societal cost. But we must not forget that abortion services also constitute an industry. In fact, it is an industry that has some very real economic and racial implications on our nation.

As the largest provider of abortion services, Planned Parenthood offers an excellent sampling of the abortion industry. Planned Parenthood cites its date of inception as 1916 when Margaret Sanger opened a birth control clinic in Brooklyn, New York.[1] Sanger, born in 1879, to a family of 11 children was a staunch advocate for women's rights. She saw the suffering of large families and the need for reproductive education. In 1923, she established the Birth Control Clinical Research Bureau and the American Birth Control League.[2] These two later merged to become Planned Parenthood Federation of America, Inc.[3]

In 2008, Planned Parenthood reported revenues of over $1 billion.[4] Government contracts and grants represented $349.6 million of that revenue, and its profits reached $85 million.[5] Planned Parenthood clinics are not performing abortions out of the goodness of their hearts. Nor do these clinics operate without the assistance of government funds. It is in Planned Parenthood's best self-interest to ensure the rate of abortions remain steady or increase.

But much more disturbing are the racial undertones within the practice of abortion. While many of her accomplishments can be commended, Planned Parenthood's founder Margaret Sanger held some radical views on the purposes of contraceptives and abortion. A 1926 article from the *Review* quotes Sanger as saying, "It now remains for the U.S. government to set a sensible example to the world by offering a bonus or yearly pension to all obviously unfit parents who allow themselves to be sterilized by

---

[1] "History & Successes." *Planned Parenthood*. Web. 17 July 2010. <http://www.plannedparenthood.org/about-us/who-we-are/history-and-successes.htm>.

[2] See "History & Successes."

[3] See "History & Successes."

[4] "Annual Report 2007-2008." *Planned Parenthood Federation of America*. Web. 17 July 2010. http://www.plannedparenthood.org/files/AR08_vFinal.pdf.

[5] See "Annual Report 2007-2008."

harmless and scientific means. In this way the moron and the diseased would have no posterity to inherit their unhappy condition."[6] In 1939, Sanger established the "Negro Project." This project discouraged reproduction by those living in poverty, especially African Americans. She recruited prestigious African Americans to help her promote the project. In October of 1939, she wrote a letter to Clarence Gamble in which she said, "The most successful educational approach to the Negro is through a religious appeal. We do not want word to go out that we want to exterminate the Negro population, and the minister is the man who can straighten out that idea if it ever occurs to any of their more rebellious members."[7]

While many supporters of Planned Parenthood undoubtedly are unaware of its somewhat racist history, Planned Parenthood still has a huge impact on minority communities today. According to the Planned Parenthood site, over 840 clinics are in operation in the U.S.. Seventy-eight percent of those clinics are in minority neighborhoods.[8] African Americans represent about 12.3 percent of the American population but have about 36 percent of all abortions.[9] Since the legalization of abortion in 1973, approximately 25 percent of the potential African American population has been lost to abortions.[10] Statistically an African American woman is three times more likely to have an abortion than a white woman.[11] The result is a staggering loss of life in the African American community.

---

[6] Green, Tanya L. "The Negro Project: Margaret Sanger's Eugenic Plan for Black Americans." *Citizenreviewonline*. 10 May 2001. Web. 17 July 2010.
http://www.citizenreviewonline.org/special_issues/population/the_ne gro_project.htm.
[7] Enouen, Susan W. "Planned Parenthood Abortion Facilities Target African American Communities." *Life Issues Institute*. n.d. Web. 17 July 2010.
<http://www.lifeissues.org/connector/display.asp?page=05oct.htm>.
[8] Piper, John. "When is Abortion Racism?" *Desiring God.* 21 Jan. 2007. Web. 17 July 2010.
http://beta.desiringgod.org/resource-library/sermons/when-is-abortion-racism.
[9] See Enouen, Susan W.
[10] See Enouen, Susan W.
[11] See Enouen, Susan W.

This unquestionably does not mean that all abortion activists are money-hungry or racist. However, the roots of abortion clinics definitely had a racist background and are negatively impacting minority communities today. However, abortion clinics as an aspect of contemporary society have suspiciously racist roots, and they are greatly impacting minority communities today. The clinics desire more than to just empower women. They are interested in turning a profit. This background and knowledge can provide some helpful insight into aspects of the abortion debate.

**Abortion and the Feminist Movement**
One of the main causes leading to widespread acceptance of abortion is the feminist movement. Today, there are feminists who identify themselves on the pro-choice and pro-life sides, but many of the non-scientific justifications for abortion find themselves rooted in feminist rhetoric. A very simple look at feminism reveals the belief that women should be privy to the same rights and opportunities as men because this will bring equality and freedom. Unfortunately, just because freedom *might* be the end result, this does not mean that it will make the lives of women any more enjoyable.

At the heart of pro-choice feminism is the desire for sexual and reproductive freedom, and an easy, tangible proof of reproductive freedom is abortion. This makes the topic of abortion paramount for feminists promoting the reproductive freedom agenda. Ellen Willis writes in *No More Nice Girls*: "Opposing abortion, then, means accepting that women must suffer sexual disempowerment and a radical loss of autonomy relative to men: if fetal life is sacred, the self-denial basic to women's oppression is also basic to the moral order."[12] This viewpoint maintains that women should be free to pursue sexual encounters for pleasure and have no fear of reproducing.

I find the arguments of pro-choice feminists flawed for three reasons. First, underlying their argument for equality is the thought that whatever makes men happy will also make women happy. Genetically, physically, and psychologically, women are very different than men. Inherently, men and women are created with different instincts. For some reason, equal treatment has morphed into the idea that truly equal and free women are those

---

[12] Ellen Willis, *No More Nice Girls*, 78.

forsaking the role of motherhood and solely pursuing a career. But for many women and men, careers are simply jobs that will never bring satisfaction. One of the great benefits of womanhood *is* the ability to reproduce. Men can never have this opportunity. Perhaps that is a prime example of inequality.

Second, I find it hard to believe that sexual freedom will bring equality for women in education or the workplace. It appears that "founding" feminists were mainly concerned with equal access for women to education and careers. With this I wholeheartedly agree. The wage disparity between women and men is still evident, and the inability of women in certain countries to even obtain an education is deplorable. However, a woman's ability to have an abortion or be free sexually will not change these problems. Yes, a woman can have an abortion and thus continue her education or career. However, it does nothing to change the existing status quo.

Finally, I find the argument that women should be allowed perfect freedom to seek pleasure flawed from the beginning. Sidney Callahan writes in "Abortion and the Sexual Agenda": "In pro-choice feminism, a permissive, erotic view of sexuality is assumed to be the only option. Sexual intercourse with a variety of partners is seen as 'inevitable' from a young age and as a positive growth experience to be managed by access to contraception and abortion."[13] Ellen Willis writes: "Opposing abortion means embracing a conservative sexual morality, one that subordinates pleasure to reproduction: if fetal life is sacred, there is no room for the view that sexual passion—or even sexual love—for its own sake is a human need and a human right."[14] Ani DiFranco, a contributor to *Abortion & Life*, takes the thought even further by stating that humans have no ability to choose abstinence. She states: "I want to tell women and men, 'You are an animal and it is a beautiful thing.'"[15] Not only is this thought demoralizing, it lowers humans to the level of animals, which is unacceptable.

If one digs into these statements, you find that abortion really is not the issue at hand. The issue is pleasure. Abortion is simply the fix for any problems resulting from the pleasure. These women want to be free to experience a variety of sexual

---

[13] Baird, *The Ethics of Abortion*, 176.
[14] Ellen Willis, *No More Nice Girls*, 78.
[15] In Baumgardner, *Abortion & Life*, 113.

encounters and not be judged by the morality of society or church. The problem is this type of "freedom" will never result in the desired freedom of mind, body, and soul or in true pleasure. Evidence of this can be seen in countless places. Juli Loesch Wiley, a former pro-choice feminist, wrote of her experiences with the sexual revolution, "I saw, first of all, that the whole 'sexual revolution' failed to live up to its claims. I began to see casualties: women ripped off by fly-by-night relationships; men and women uneasily aware that they'd used somebody, or that they'd *been* used."[16] She saw the resulting emotions of pain, emptiness, and numbness. King Solomon provides another example of the emptiness of materialistic pleasures. Solomon had more wealth and wisdom than any other man in the history of the world, and he sought every pleasure known to man. Yet, he wrote in Ecclesiastes 2:10-11, "I denied myself nothing my eyes desired; I refused my heart no pleasure. My heart took delight in all my work, and this was the reward for all my labor. Yet when I surveyed all that my hands had done and what I had toiled to achieve, everything was meaningless, a chasing after the wind; nothing was gained under the sun."

In the thought bubble of a pro-choice feminist, the right to an abortion represents freedom and access to limitless pleasure. In reality, however, abortion brings neither.

**Abortion and Personhood**
A surprising aspect of the abortion debate I have thus far been exposed to is the general consensus of philosophical minds that the fetus is alive and is human. This is surprising because it seems to be an argument of great concern to the largely-uninformed audience. Yes, there are some who debate this topic, but the argument typically revolves around the "personhood" of the fetus rather than its humanity. According to a 1990 Gallup poll, 76 percent of respondents believed that abortion was the taking of another human life.[17]

Scientific advancements are a large reason that the life of a fetus is no longer a primary point of conflict. Bernard Nathanson, a pro-choice leader in the 1960s and 1970s who is now a pro-life advocate, points this out: "There is no longer serious doubt in my mind that human life exists within the womb from

---

[16] Juli Loesch Wiley, "Solidarity and Shalom," in Tickle, ed., 43.
[17] Frederica Mathewes-Green, *Real Choices*, 20.

the very onset of pregnancy, despite the fact that the nature of the intrauterine life has been the subject of considerable dispute in the past."[18]

Even many pro-choice activists do not hesitate to affirm the humanity of the fetus. Naomi Wolf, a pro-choice advocate, writes, "Sometimes the mother must be able to decide that the fetus, in its full humanity, must die."[19] She appears to try to lessen the blow of this statement by also saying, "But it is never right or necessary to minimize the value of the lives involved or the sacrifice incurred in letting them go."[20] These statements are extremely difficult to rationalize. First, Wolf declares that a fetus has full humanity. Then she makes the claim that the mother can decide if this fetus, with full humanity, should or should not die. Is there any other instance in life when one human being can decide to take the life of another? Aside from the institution of the death penalty, which is an entirely different circumstance, I can think of no other. In any other situation, this would be defined as murder. Wolf further states that aborted babies should be remembered by "passionate feminists" who "hold candlelight vigils at abortion clinics, standing shoulder to shoulder with the doctors who work there, commemorating and saying goodbye to the dead."[21] The irony of this argument is astounding.

Because it is hard for abortion centrists to swallow the reasoning of those like Wolf, many pro-choice advocates shift the debate to the personhood of the fetus. *This* is not a scientific question but rather one of reasoning and philosophy. While the distinction between humanity and personhood might seem to be a matter of semantics at first, it is a matter of great importance to many. If the personhood of a fetus cannot be established, the fetus arguably has no rights, thus making the woman more important in all scenarios. After all, Jefferson wrote that all "men" are created equal and are endowed with unalienable rights. If it can be proven that a fetus is not a "person" then some believe moral rights and the Bill of Rights do not apply.

Mary Anne Warren contributes significantly to this debate in her article "On the Moral and Legal Status of Abortion." In this

---

[18] Bernard Nathanson, *Aborting America*, 165.
[19] In Baird, *The Ethics of Abortion*, 187.
[20] In Baird, *The Ethics of Abortion*, 187.
[21] In Baird, *The Ethics of Abortion*, 192.

article Warren sets forth five seemingly reasonable traits of a person. They are "(1) consciousness (of objects and events external and/or internal to the being), and in particular the capacity to feel pain; (2) reasoning (the *developed* capacity to solve new and relatively complex problems); (3) self-motivated activity (activity which is relatively independent of either genetic or direct external control); (4) the capacity to communicate, by whatever means, messages of an indefinite variety of types, that is, not just with an indefinite number of possible contents, but on indefinitely many possible topics; (5) the presence of self-concepts, and self-awareness, either individual or racial, or both."[22] According to Warren, a fetus obviously can fulfill none of these traits and, thus, is not a person. She further states, "I consider this claim to be so obvious that I think anyone who denied it, and claimed that a being which satisfied none of (1)-(5) was a person all the same, would thereby demonstrate that he had no notion at all of what a person is—perhaps because he had confused the concept of a person with that of genetic humanity."[23]

Following these guidelines for determining personhood and, more importantly, the right to moral and constitutional rights is dangerous. First, it cannot be scientifically proven that a fetus cannot communicate and is not conscious of internal and external events. A baby can cry in the womb. At 51-53 days, an embryo can move spontaneously, and at 24 weeks, a fetus can respond to a stimulus (light and sound) whether it is from an outside or inside source. In her zealous attempt to deny a fetus any rights, Warren rejects even the *potential* personhood of a fetus taking a single snap-shot at a single moment in time to determine that a fetus is not a person. She does not consider the rapid development of a fetus or determine when a fetus or baby can be considered a person. Perhaps, personhood could more appropriately be determined over the flow of time. Second, if this litmus test for personhood is applied across the board, adults who are mentally retarded, grandparents with Alzheimer's disease, and individuals in comas could be considered "non-persons." Following the reasoning that a fetus is not a person and should not have any rights, these situations would also result in the loss of rights for individuals once considered people but

---

[22] In Baird, *The Ethics of Abortion*, 274-75.
[23] In Baird, *The Ethics of Abortion*, 275.

degraded to the status of animals. The implications of this argument balance precariously on the precipice of eugenics.

In the end, this attempt to shift the argument from humanity to personhood and, thus, rights appears to be an attempt to muddle the argument and is a moot point. The debate of life and personhood is an affront to God. God is the Creator and Sustainer of all things, and humans have the unique distinction amongst all creation of being created in the very image of God. God knows the person from the instant of creation, even before. Psalm 139:13 states, "For you created my inmost being; you knit me together in my mother's womb."

Of course, this does not answer the question of why—why does a young girl who is raped become pregnant? How could God allow this to happen? Surely God did not mean for *this* child to be created. I cannot answer why the horrible sin happened. But I can say that God was fully aware that this child would be created because He is sovereign. Ecclesiastes 11:5 affirms, "As you do not know the path of the wind, or how the body is formed in a mother's womb, so you cannot understand the work of God, the Maker of all things."

The issue is not the rights of the mother versus the rights of the fetus. The issue is the life of a baby that God, in His sovereignty, is creating. Are the created so wise that they can tell the Creator when He has made a mistake?

## Abortion and Choices

Regardless of where one falls on the abortion debate, most would seem to agree that abortions happen far too often. According to the Second Look Project, 1.29 million abortions were performed in 2002, which brought the total to 42 million legal abortions since 1973.[24] A pregnancy in the U.S. has a 24.5 percent chance of ending in an abortion, and the U.S. boasts the highest rate of abortion among developed countries.[25] These statistics are staggering.

Understanding that abortions will not stop whether they are legal or illegal makes it imperative to offer women choices. Frederica Mathewes-Green writes in *Real Choices*, "No one wants an abortion as she wants an ice-cream cone or a Porsche.

---

[24] "Statistics." *The Second Look Project.* n.d. Web. 17 July 2010. <http://www.secondlookproject.org/tslp_stats.html>.
[25] See "Statistics."

She wants an abortion as an animal, caught in a trap, wants to gnaw off its own leg."[26] Mathewes-Green continues that the majority of women are not singing and dancing on the way to the abortion clinic. In fact, most abortions happen because of pressure from outside factors. It is *not* an empowering choice made by the woman alone. The Reardon Case Studies included in *Real Choices* list the top four reasons that women have abortions as 1) pressure from the husband or partner, 2) a lack of information or confusion, 3) pressure from parents, and 4) a lack of alternatives.[27]

Unfortunately, reasons 1 and 3 are very difficult to combat. Mathewes-Green commented that her discussions with women revealed that, "In nearly every case, the abortion was undertaken to fulfill a felt obligation to another person, a parent or boyfriend."[28] Without the influence of unrelated parties, it is foreseeable that these situations would end in an abortion.

This is where alternatives and choices can come into play. First, pregnancy care centers can offer women hope in hopeless situations. The centers counsel women on finances, housing, and other logistical matters, but, most importantly, they can provide the love and support that many women are yearning for. Second, churches should take an active role in helping support mothers who choose to keep their babies even in undesirable circumstances. The silent role of the church body as a whole in this area is shameful. Yes, churches are quick to condemn abortions. But they are rarely quick to provide the support a young mother who chooses life or abortion needs. This does not mean that they need to condone situations that led to the pregnancy, but a showing of love and grace from the church is crucial. After all, Christ did not come to save the righteous but the sinners. The church, full of sinners saved only by God's grace, should know this best of all.

An ideal choice for many mothers is adoption. A 1991 Gallup poll revealed that 82 percent of respondents believed adoption was a better solution than abortion.[29] Yet, this is a difficult choice for many mothers to make. Only about 1 percent of women who are unintentionally pregnant choose adoption.[30] As Mathewes-

---

[26] Mathewes-Green, *Real Choices*, 11.
[27] Mathewes-Green, *Real Choices*, 208.
[28] Mathewes-Green, *Real Choices*, 22.
[29] Mathewes-Green, *Real Choices*, 101.

Green points out, "The woman seems to face two impossible alternatives: I can't raise this child and I can't stand letting it go—so I'll just erase it."[31] Most reading that quote would recognize the illogical and selfish reasoning. However, *most* reading the statement are not in the situation. Women must be encouraged to look beyond their own desires and their own selfishness to think of the baby. Through these options women can be assured of making the best possible choice.

## Abortion and its Effects

The most impactful abortion testimonial I have read is that of Bernard Nathanson. After performing thousands of abortions, Nathanson came to the firm resolution that abortion was murder. Even though he subsequently dedicated his life to the pro-life movement, he could not lose the guilt of his actions. He said, "I despise myself."[32] Finally, he found rest in the only One who could take his burden and fling it as far as the east is from the west.

Abortion is destructive. It is destructive because it does not provide the freedom that feminists desire. It does not empower; it does not equalize genders. It does not solve the debate between rights of the mother and rights of the fetus. It merely glosses over the Biblical and historical significance of a life in order to provide a quick solution for a difficult situation.

But most importantly, abortion impacts lives. It impacts the lives of women, men, and fetuses. Countless women attest to the great burdens, like Nathanson's burden, they have carried after having an abortion. Life is too important to be burdened and destroyed by abortion.

The abortion debate will inevitably continue for as long as the earth exists. The complexity of life will ensure this. However, it is imperative for the health of our nation and the world that better options are available for unplanned pregnancies. Only then will women and men find the empowerment and fulfillment they are so desperately seeking.

---

[30] Mathewes-Green, *Real Choices*, 103.
[31] Mathewes-Green, *Real Choices*, 104.
[32] Nathanson, *The Hand of God*, 190.

CHAPTER FIVE

Abortion and the Drama of Human Motivations:
With Reference to Kenneth Burke and René Girard

by Charles Bellinger

For those who are unfamiliar with Kenneth Burke, I will present a thumbnail biography. He was born in 1897 and died in 1993. He attended Columbia University for one semester, but then dropped out of college and became a self-educated thinker by reading voraciously and interacting with the intelligentsia in the New York City area. In his earlier years as an author he was a music and literature critic; he gradually morphed into a philosopher, with a strong interest in anthropology. Politically, he was sympathetic with Marxism, but not in an overly narrow and doctrinaire way. His main books are: *Counter-Statement* (1931), *Permanence and Change* (1935), *Attitudes Toward History* (1937), *The Philosophy of Literary Form* (1941), *A Grammar of Motives* [GM] (1945), *A Rhetoric of Motives* [RM] (1950), *The Rhetoric of Religion* (1961), and *Language as Symbolic Action* [LSA] (1966). He also wrote one novel, and some works of short fiction and poetry. Burke is primarily studied today in English and Speech departments as a major twentieth century theoretician of rhetoric. There is a Kenneth Burke Society which holds a conference every three years.

Many readers of René Girard are probably under the impression that Girard coined the phrase "the scapegoat mechanism." Actually, Burke was already using that phrase in *Permanence and Change* in 1935. There is also a section of *A Grammar of Motives* entitled "The Dialectic of the Scapegoat." In various places in his writings Burke spoke of violence toward scapegoats as an act of psychological catharsis this serves the end of social cohesion. From the few scattered references to Burke in Girard's writings, it is clear that Burke had a significant influence on Girard, though the way Girard formulated the concepts of mimetic desire, scapegoating, and biblical revelation took him into territory that Burke did not enter himself. Burke described himself as an agnostic, though he was not at all hostile toward religious ideas or religious people. One of his key late works was *The Rhetoric of Religion*, which includes extensive comment-aries on Genesis chapters 1-3 and on Augustine's *Confessions*.

It is fair to say that Burke and Girard are similar in that they are known primarily as anthropologists, not as ethicists. By this I mean that they both tend to steer clear of making direct comments on the topics that ethicists talk about: just war theory vs. pacifism, abortion, genetic manipulation, and so forth. It does not follow, however, that there are no ethical ideas or implications embedded within their writings. I believe that Burke and Girard chose to focus on anthropology because they had deeply felt ethical concerns that could not be adequately addressed using the language of ethics *per se*. One can argue about just war theories and pacifism without asking the deeper question: Why are human beings violent? Burke and Girard both intuitively sense that in the modern world clashing ideologies cannot find peace if there is simply a war of competing ethical *answers*. We need to be asking deeper anthropological *questions*. Hence, Burke's main concern became comprehending human *motives*, and Girard continued that same train of thought, though along a somewhat different track.

Some people accuse Girard of having too much of a "grand meta-narrative." In my opinion, Girard's meta-narrative is not grand enough. I contend that we need a complex anthropological vision that outlines how human beings inhabit the various dimensions of reality. There is the vertical axis of God and nature, traditionally called the Great Chain of Being. There is the horizontal plane of human social relations. And there is individual human selfhood in time. The dimensions are fields within reality that can be described through the use of clusters of words.

- The vertical axis evokes words such as hierarchy, monarchy, spirit and matter, divine law and natural law, idolatry, master and slave, love of God, the eternal and the temporal, natural evil
- The horizontal plane evokes words such as democracy, diversity, equality, solidarity, a mob mentality and scapegoating, love of neighbor, moral evil
- The trajectory of individual selfhood evokes words such

> as inwardness, individualism, imagination, free will, narcissism, autonomy, love of self, growth in virtue, temptation to (individual) evil

These lists are not exhaustive, of course, just suggestive.

I say that Girard's meta-narrative is not grand enough because Girard's thought is a masterful exposition of the horizontal plane, but it focuses too narrowly on that dimension of reality. Kierkegaard is a thinker who focuses on individual selfhood; Aquinas focuses on the vertical axis. Thinkers often have a forté, a powerful vision of a particular aspect of reality which they develop with great skill and power. But my plea is that we should always be expanding our vision to comprehend the widest possible circumference of elements. Of course, Girard, Kierkegaard, and Aquinas are aware of all three key dimensions of reality, but the question I'm raising concerns how successfully a thinker holds the dimensions in a creative tension and synthesis.

This concept of complex dimensional anthropology had already come into focus for me, based on reading Eric Voegelin, Kierkegaard, Girard, and other thinkers, before I started reading Kenneth Burke, and I was gratified to see that he was wrestling with the exact same problem. When he wrote his central philosophical work, *A Grammar of Motives*, he had in mind that this would be the first book of a trilogy. The second would be *A Rhetoric of Motives* and the third *A Symbolic of Motives*. What did Burke mean by grammar, rhetoric, and symbolic, which are obviously his key terms?

By grammar, Burke means reflection on the ontological basis of human life, the substance of human beings. He points out that the word "substance" is paradoxical; its root meaning, sub-stance, is that which lies underneath something, the ground on which the thing is standing. For human beings, our substance in this sense is our physical embodiedness—the bones, muscles, blood, and DNA that constitute our physical life. But the word substance is paradoxical in that it is usually used to indicate the essence of something, its internal spirit or soul. The substance of a person is both their (material) brain and also their (immaterial) mind or intellect. By rhetoric, Burke means "persuasion and dissuasion, communication and polemic." Rhetoric is the use of language to form and sustain a community, usually by verbally attacking some other community or some group within the community. "The *Rhetoric* deals with the possibilities of classification in its *partisan* aspects; it considers the ways in which individuals are at odds with one another, or become identified with groups more or less at odds with one another." By symbolic, Burke means reflection on a thing's *identity*, "its uniqueness as an entity in itself and by itself." The symbolic perspective treats "the individual substances, or entities, or constituted acts . . . considered in their uniqueness"(RM, 21-23). So we can see that Burke saw clearly the dimensional anthropology that I outlined above. The terms grammar and substance correspond with what I'm calling the vertical axis; rhetoric corresponds with the horizontal plane; and symbolic corresponds with individual selfhood in its uniqueness.

Burke also identifies a cluster of three terms that reinforce this analysis: "Order, the Secret, and the Kill" (RM, 265). He describes these as three key motives around which human life in society revolve. By *order*, Burke means the hierarchies of human society that mirror the hierarchy of lower and higher life forms in nature. By *the secret*, Burke means the interiority of the human person, who is deciding to act. By *the kill*, he means scapegoating and sacrifice.

I don't have time within the limited scope of this paper to adequately expand this point, but in the writings of Søren Kierkegaard and Eric Voegelin, I see an awareness of dimensional anthropology articulated with great subtlety and philosophical depth.[1] They portray the human self as existing at the intersection of the dimensions of reality. Our sinfulness, our malformation, as human beings, is our inability, or refusal, to faithfully synthesize the dimensions and hold them in creative tension as we live our lives before God. Burke and Girard don't put things in this precise way, but I see them as presenting anthropological visions that arise out of similar intuitions about the health and sickness of human beings. Burke's overall project is to articulate the complexity of human motivational derailments as a failure to synthesize grammar, symbolism, and rhetoric in an ethical way. Girard's overall project is to show how human beings fail to find true selfhood when they are swept up in the social dynamics of mimetic desire and scapegoating. Living exclusively on the horizontal plane is an "ontological sickness" that can only be healed by one thing, by entering into

---

[1] See Charles Bellinger, *The Trinitarian Self: The Key to the Puzzle of Violence.*

43

the kingdom of God, into good mimesis. True *selfhood* is found in relation to the *God* who is revealed in Christ. The vertical, selfhood, and the social then cooperate in a healthy way.

When the dimensions of reality come into focus for us, we can see that the primary examples of unethical behavior in the modern world fall along dimensional lines. The defense of slavery in the 19th century, for example, arose out of vertical othering, the idea that whites are superior to blacks in the Great Chain of Being. Slavery was an example of what Burke called a "hierarchical psychosis." The Nazis and the Stalinists engaged in horizontal othering. They used rhetoric to label certain human beings as belonging to groups that needed to be eliminated. They overemphasized the horizontal plane and its organ of power the State. They refused to respect the dignity and value of individual human beings. In our age extreme individualism tends to overemphasize selfhood, which leads to other forms of pathology. When we see that the dimensions are temptations to overemphasis that can lead to unjust violence, then an ethical imperative will naturally present itself to us: we ought to live in the Center, holding the dimensions in a balanced and creative synthesis.

This analysis allows us to make some comments on the abortion debate. Let us consider Burke's dramatic pentad as an illustration of the difficulty involved in this question. (Burke's pentad employs the terms Scene, Agent, Act, Agency, and Purpose to analyze the drama of human life in literature and in history. GM, xvii) For example, one could comment on the abortion debate by saying that pro-choice advocates place the emphasis on the Agent and view the fetus in Scenic terms, as natural matter that is lower down on the Great Chain of Being. The Act of abortion, using suction technology as an Agency is morally appropriate in a particular circumstance given the Purposes of the woman, her plans for the future unfolding of her life. Pro-life advocates, on the other hand, think that it is wrong to view the unborn child as mere matter, as impersonal substance; rather, the unborn child should be treated as an Agent-in-formation (with "rights"). Alternatively, God should be seen as the Agent who is creating the child and abortion is destroying God's work. In either case, the Agent-Scene ratio is interpreted differently than it is by pro-choice advocates, who use the language of individual autonomy to place more emphasis on the woman as Agent. It follows from the pro-life assumptions that the use of abortive technology is morally wrong because the Purposes for which it is being employed are not appropriate from the pro-life point of view. A woman should be open to adjusting her life to receive a child (or give up the child for adoption) instead of controlling her future through an Act that is viewed as unjust violence.[2] Burke's term "circumference" can also be useful here. For Burke, circumference or scope are terms that indicate how broad or narrow a person's philosophical perception of the Scene is. Pro-choice advocates commonly speak about the circumstances of a particular woman's life—her financial resources, her relationships or lack thereof, her employment situation, her health, etc. Pro-life advocates commonly talk about abortion in connection with slavery and the Holocaust, by claiming that the fetus is "owned" by the woman as a slave-owner owned slaves, and that the fetus is dehumanized in pro-choice rhetoric just as Hitler dehumanized the Jews.[3] This sort of accusatory rhetoric sounds bizarre and offensive to pro-choice ears. Looked at from Burke's point of view, the difference in perspectives arise out of two disparate circumferences: a focus on the particular situation of a woman vs. placing abortion within the broad Scene of modern history. As Burke says: "the choice of circumference for the scene in terms of which a given act is to be located will have a corresponding effect upon the interpretation of the act itself"(GM, 77).

Neither Burke nor Girard include in their published writings a lengthy commentary on the abortion debate. It is possible that a person could study their writings thoroughly and then affirm either a pro-choice or a pro-life stance. However, I think that the moral arc of the analysis bends in a pro-life direction. The pro-choice position, for example, is usually presented as a set of nested propositions: 1) the sovereign political principle relating to abortion ought to be the complete autonomy of the individual self, 2) the natural fertility of a woman's body is perceived as threatening, because it can "enslave" a woman to her biology, 3) pro-lifers seek to impose their moral beliefs on others, limiting

---

[2] For another discussion of the pentad and abortion, see Stan A. Lindsay, *Implicit Rhetoric: Kenneth Burke's Extension of Aristotle's Concept of Entelechy* (New York: University Press of America, 1998), 111-28.
[3] See, for example, James Burtchaell, *Rachel Weeping and Other Essays on Abortion* (New York: Andrews and McMeel, 1982), 141-287.

the liberty of those others, 4) if this social imposition is enforced by the State, principle #1 is contradicted, 5) abortion is morally acceptable because the fetus is natural matter, not a "person" possessing rights, until some later point in time (viability, birth, or after birth, according to various arguments). From the perspective of the dimensional anthropology outlined above, this picture just painted is an example of overemphasizing the individual self within the overall complexity of reality. In a key passage in *A Grammar of Motives* (364), Burke points out that seeing the individual as alienated from and threatened by society is a particular feature of the modern west. In earlier centuries, when there was a more organic understanding of human beings participating in society, the individual was seen as a microcosm that is part of a macrocosm. But in more recent times, it is common for people to define themselves as individuals over against society. Now we have "the individual *against* the group," in that any curb on the absolute freedom of the individual will is a case of society tyrannically imposing its will on the individual. Burke says that in this modern development a "fall" has taken place. Burke is not recommending extreme individualism as a good thing; he is placing it in a dubious light. He implies that there is a need for a "wider circumference" which takes into account the social, natural, or supernatural environment in general, rather than saying that the individual trumps everything else in the universe (GM, 362). In his important essay entitled "Definition of Man," he speaks of human beings as separated from their "natural condition by instruments of their own making"(LSA, 3-24). This can be seen as a critique of the idea that the natural fertility of a woman's body is an alien force which must be controlled by the technology of abortion.[4]

Burke uses the term "transubstantiation" to describe a historical period in which the "substance" of the political life of a people undergoes a major upheaval (GM, 320). The American Revolution, for example, was a transubstantiation from a monarchical political structure that is vertical, to a democratic political structure that is horizontal. *Roe v. Wade*, we can suggest, was another major upheaval that accomplished a transubstantiation from horizontal democracy to individual selfhood as the preeminent source of sovereignty.[5] But *Roe v.*

---

[4] See also John Wilcox, "Nature as Demonic in Thomson's Defense of Abortion," in Baird, *The Ethics of Abortion*.

*Wade* is so controversial precisely because so many people either think that this transubstantiation was an error, or that narrowing the scope of sovereignty to one dimension of life is an error.

Girard's thought also bends toward the pro-life view, as we can see when he refers to abortion as a modern return to ancient "pagan practices."[6] This case is made compellingly by Bernadette Waterman Ward in a *Contagion* article.[7] She argues that the rhetoric of "pro-choice" does not correlate in a truthful way with the psychological reality of women in contemporary American culture. Echoing Girard's idea that modern "autonomy" is an illusion, she argues that abortions are sought not because women are autonomous but precisely because they are *not*. Women are enmeshed in a male-dominated sexual and economic milieu which treats them as objects of sexual desire that must conform to that milieu. Immense pressure is often put on a woman to have an abortion by various other persons in her life; or she may put pressure on herself because of a perception that the child she is carrying is a threat to the dream of economic success in a materialistic society that she has been mimetically conformed to. Instead of transforming the cultural system that oppresses women and denigrates their capacity to bring life into the world, the ideology of abortion treats the unborn child as a threat who must be sacrificed in order to conservatively perpetuate the male dominated system of structural violence.

In sum, I have argued that dimensional anthropology greatly illuminates various aspects of human behavior in the modern world. The dimensions are sources of "temptation" in that they can be overemphasized, resulting in an unbalanced way of inhabiting reality, which lays the foundation for various forms of unjust violence. Slavery was predicated on vertical othering. There are many forms of horizontal othering, such as Nazism, Stalinism, and the ethnic violence in Rwanda and Yugoslavia. Abortion is a form of temporal othering in which it is claimed that the fetus may be killed because it is "not yet" a person.[8] This

---

[5] See Jean Bethke Elshtain, *Sovereignty: God, State, and Self* (New York: Basic Books, 2008).

[6] René Girard, *I See Satan Fall Like Lightning* (Maryknoll, NY: Orbis, 2001), 181.

[7] Bernadette Waterman Ward, "Abortion as a Sacrament: Mimetic Desire and Sacrifice in Sexual Politics." *Contagion: Journal of Violence, Mimesis & Culture* 7 (2000): 18-35.

[8] See Mary Ann Warren, "On the Moral and Legal Status of Abortion," in

form of othering arises out of an overemphasis on individual selfhood, a mistake that is implicitly and explicitly critiqued by Kenneth Burke and René Girard. The self exists in time, but the Golden Rule is broken when the temporal existence of a born individual is recognized and valued, while the temporal existence of the unborn child is seen as a fit subject for the type of sacrificial violence that perpetuates an unjust and immature social order. The various forms of othering that lead to unjust violence are always in direct opposition to the Golden Rule: "So whatever you wish that men would do to you, do so to them; for this is the law and the prophets."(Matt. 7:12)

---

Baird, *The Ethics of Abortion*, 276.

CHAPTER SIX

Abortion: A Christian Perspective

by Walter Braddock

In this sermon I will address the issue of abortion from a Christian perspective, mainly for a United Methodist congregation. I realize there are many avenues and special cases that I will not address in detail. I will not speak to abortion in relation to rape, incest, abortion to save the mother's life, or abortion due to fetal abnormality even though these are certainly important issues in the abortion debate. But in the space permitted, I will seek to bring our biblical and theological resources into view, hoping to find common ground with which to stand as God's people living in a fallen world, and all the while being surrounded by God's marvelous grace wooing us into a relationship.

**Introduction**
On January 22, 1973, the US Supreme Court handed down the most enduringly controversial Court decision of the century, and it is still one of the most debated topics in America today. The case was *Roe v Wade*. Norma McCorvey of Dallas County, Texas, who had assumed the name Jane Roe to protect her identity, sued the state of Texas for the right to have a legal and safe elective abortion. Up to this point, abortions were only legal in Texas in order to save the life of the mother, but elective abortions (those not medically required) were against the law:

> Roe alleged that she was unmarried and pregnant; that she wished to terminate her pregnancy by an abortion "performed by a competent, licensed physician, under safe, clinical conditions"; that she was unable to get a "legal" abortion in Texas because her life did not appear to be threatened by the continuation of the pregnancy;

and that she could not afford to travel to another jurisdiction in order to secure a legal abortion under safe conditions (Baird, *The Ethics of Abortion*, 63-64).

Roe's attorneys asked the Supreme Court to find the Texas abortion laws unconstitutional based upon the Ninth and Fourteenth amendments to the Constitution. At the time, elective abortion was illegal in forty-six of our fifty states.

In its simplest form, the *Roe* decision stated that the right to terminate a pregnancy is a matter of personal decision and is a privacy issue protected by the Constitution. On the day after *Roe*, women suddenly had a constitutional right to get an abortion for any reason, a right that effectively applied at any time during the nine months of pregnancy. Since that time, the number of abortions quickly soared to almost 1.5 million every year, roughly 30 percent of all pregnancies (McConnell, 135). Now there have been over 40 million abortions in the U.S. alone. Abortion is legal, just as slavery was legal in the 1800s - an issue that split the Methodist Church in her darkest hour. But, is abortion moral? What does the Bible say on the subject?

**Biblical View**
Nowhere in the Bible does it say, "Thou shall not commit abortion." Neither does it specifically mention many other moral issues, but the Bible does speak about life and death, and before life and beyond death, as well as living in between these times. Since the Bible is not specific, good Christians from many denominations and independent churches alike, which includes United Methodists, will have many different views about abortion and how the Bible relates to it.

The text I want to begin with today is from Psalm 139:13-16:

"For it was you who formed my inward parts; you knit me together in my mother's womb. I praise you, for I am fearfully and wonderfully made. Wonderful are your works; that I know very well. My frame was not hidden from you, when I was being made in secret, intricately woven in the depths of the earth. Your eyes beheld my unformed substance. In your book were written all the days that were formed for me, when none of them as yet existed."

According to the Bible, God knew each of us before we were born. In fact, before we are even formed in the womb, God knows us. God knows how each day of our lives on earth will unfold and who we will become. The prophet Jeremiah also uses this poetic language when he describes his call from God, "Now the word of the Lord came to me saying, 'Before I formed you in the womb I knew you, and before you were born I consecrated you . . .'" (Jer. 1:4-5). Again, in Isaiah 49:5 we hear similar language, "And now the Lord says, who formed me in the womb to be his servant, to bring Jacob back to him, and that Israel might be gathered to him, for I am honored in the sight of the Lord . . . ."

In his sermon, *Life in the Tragic Dimension: A Sermon on Abortion*, Roger A. Paynter argues that even though these passages are poetic expressions of the truth that God is the Creator and the source of all creative processes, and they should instill in us a reverence toward all life, unborn as well as born, they should not be used as proof of when, in the complex physical, spiritual process of creation, fetal life becomes human personhood (in Baird, 235). I agree with Paynter, but like many pro-choice advocates, I believe he is caught up in the "personhood of the fetus" debate. For me, the point the verses are trying to express is that life begins before birth. These verses show that we are in relationship with God our Creator before we are born. God has breathed into us the breath of life and we became living beings (Gen. 2:7). God has gone into great detail in forming us, molding us, and fashioning us into the people God has ordained us to be - if allowed to live by human moral standards. These passages certainly contain several different contexts and were meant for different audiences at different times, and there are many others I could have chosen. The point is that God is in relationship with the unborn. God is the one who gives life. To end the life would be murder (Exod. 20:13).

But pro-choice advocates do not agree. In his essay "Why Abortion Is Immoral," Don Marquis explains that pro-choicers argue against these claims; that fetuses are not persons or that fetuses are not rational agents or that fetuses are not social beings. Pro-choicers believe that abortion is not wrongful killing because "being a person is what gives an individual intrinsic moral worth" and a fetus is not a person (in Baird, 310).

As noted, much of the abortion debate is over this issue of personhood. The Constitution does not define "person" in so many words. In *Roe v. Wade*, the observation of the courts revealed that the word "person," as used in the Fourteenth Amendment, does not include the unborn. They continue to say:

> We need not resolve the difficult question of when life begins. When those trained in the respective disciplines of medicine, philosophy, and theology are unable to arrive at any consensus, the judiciary, at this point in the development of man's knowledge, is not in a position to speculate as to the answer. It should be sufficient to note briefly the wide divergence of thinking on this most sensitive and difficult question. There has always been strong support for the view that life does not begin until live birth (Baird, *The Ethics of Abortion*, 68).

Ecclesiastes 11:5 speaks of our limited knowledge on this topic, but speaks in the sense that life happens whether we understand it or not. The writer says, "Just as you do not know how the breath comes to the bones in the mother's womb, so you do not know the work of God, who makes everything." Luke 1:36-42 describes Mary visiting Elizabeth while Elizabeth was in her sixth month of pregnancy with John the Baptist. When Elizabeth heard Mary's voice, John leaps in his mother's womb, a sign Elizabeth takes to mean that the Holy Spirit has prompted even this unborn child at the visit of Mary and the child Jesus in her womb. I find it interesting that medicine, philosophy and theology cannot agree on when life begins, when scientific facts show that the head and internal organs have formed and the baby's heart has been beating since the end of the fourth week.

At the time John the Baptist responded to the Holy Spirit at six months in the womb he had a face, body, arms, legs, fingers, eyes, ears, and hair. He even had fingerprints that were unique to him. He had eyelids that would open and close. He was able to grab hold of objects. But according to the Courts and pro-choice advocates, John the Baptist was not considered a person at this point and he had no rights, because, as a fetus, he was not considered "viable," that is, potentially able to live outside the mother's womb, albeit with artificial aid. Viability is usually placed at about seven months.

Another well-known text that is used by pro-life advocates to express the value of an unborn child is Exodus 21:22. In this text the Law states, "When two people who are fighting injure a pregnant woman so that there is a miscarriage, and yet no further harm follows, the one responsible shall be fined what the woman's husband demands, paying as much as the judge determines." Pro-choice advocates also use this text continuing with verse twenty-three that states, "If any harm follows (meaning to the mother), then you shall give life for life, eye for eye, tooth for tooth, hand for hand, foot for foot ..." They stress the lack of value placed on the unborn child which only warrants a fine compared to the value of the mother which warrants an equal punishment, even a life if the woman dies.

In the essay "Christians and Abortion," Richard Schoenig stresses that many Jewish scholars suggest that this passage from Exodus says that the fetus should not be considered morally a human, but later the Septuagint (Greek version of the Hebrew Bible) presented Exodus 21:22 somewhat differently. It states that if the fetus was "formed" the penalty was capital punishment, but if "unformed" it was again a fine (in Baird, 228). I am not sure how they determined between "formed" and "unformed" in this early day and time, but it is obvious that the personhood debate continues.

**Tradition**
Looking at Church tradition from its earliest time reveals that the Christian view on abortion was that it was a grave sin at any stage of development. But by the third and fourth centuries Latin church fathers such as Jerome and Augustine held that abortion is not homicide until the "scattered elements" are formed into a body, which brings up the personhood debate all over again. Clement of Alexandria, who lived about A.D. 200, said that abortion destroyed what God had created and was an offense against the command to love our neighbor (Hamilton, *Confronting the Controversies*, 121).

While speaking to the Taskforce of United Methodists on Abortion and Sexuality, Stanley Hauerwas, Professor of Theological Ethics at Duke University Divinity School, challenged a group of Methodists to reconsider the problem of abortion from within the faith and life of the Church. One of Hauerwas' main arguments focuses on this "personhood" debate which seems to have America stuck. He says:

> It is odd for Christians to take this approach since we believe that we are first of all citizens of a far different kingdom than something called the United States of

America. If we end up identifying persons with the ability to reason—which, I think, finally renders all of our lives deeply problematic—then we cannot tell why it is that we ought to care for the profoundly retarded. One of the most chilling aspects of the current abortion debate in the wider society is the general acceptance, even among anti-abortion people, of the legitimacy of aborting severely defective children. Where do people get that idea? Where do people get the idea that severely defective children are somehow a less valuable gift from God? People get that idea by privileging rationality. We privilege our ability to reason. I find that morally indefensible.

We must remember that as Christians we do not believe in the inherent sacredness of life or in personhood. Instead, we believe that that there is much worth dying for. Christians do not believe that life is a right or that we have inherent dignity. Instead, we believe that life is the gift of a gracious God ("Abortion, Theologically Understood," in *The Hauerwas Reader*, 615-16).

Hauerwas and Clement are almost on the same page. As Christians, we must change our focus from "non-personhood" in order to justify abortion toward reaching out to those who have to make tough decisions about life and about death in today's world.

The United Methodist Church believes that the beginning of life and the ending of life are the God-given boundaries of human existence. Through advanced technology humanity now has some degree of control and power over those who die and the life of those who are unborn. This control and this power comes with a great responsibility for the sanctity of human life. The United Methodist Church respects this sacredness of the life and well-being of the mother and the unborn child. When tragic conflicts of life with life occur, The United Methodist Church recognizes that the legal option of abortion under proper medical procedures may be justifiable. The United Methodist Church does not however, affirm abortion as an acceptable means of birth control, which is the primary reason for most abortions that are performed today, and unconditionally rejects abortion as a means of gender selection (The Book of Discipline of the United Methodist Church, 2008, 105).

## Conclusion

God is in the creation business and has called humanity to be partners in that creating process. As Christians we are to love our neighbors as ourselves. We are to love one another as Christ loved each of us. What does it mean to love? Paul D. Simmons brings out an interesting point when he explains objectively that the fetus is not a person because it has not acquired the capacities or characteristics that define an entity as a person. But subjectively, the pregnant woman or the couple in question may regard the conceptus as a person and provide it with all the respect and protection a person should be accorded. He continues to explain that it is not vitality but the acceptance, affirmation, recognition and love of the fetus that grants personhood and assures that it will become a person (Simmons, 214).

Adam Hamilton also recognizes this interesting fact and notes that those who oppose abortion point out that the unborn child is called a "baby" when we want the child but a "fetus" when we do not want the child. How can this be, they wonder? It is the same child. Does our desire for the child make it a baby, while our rejection makes it a fetus (Hamilton, 118)? Love and care does make a difference in the way we see and experience life. As stewards of God's creation, and as priests ("you are a chosen people, a royal priesthood, a holy nation, God's special possession, that you may declare the praises of him who called you out of darkness into his wonderful light,"1 Peter 2:9) it is our responsibility to provide that love and care to all beings, born and unborn.

When Adam Hamilton asked his 13,000 member congregation to send in stories of women who have faced a decision concerning abortion, one in particular stood out. The woman shared that when she was seventeen she became pregnant. When her father found out about the pregnancy, he was furious. This was the days before *Roe v. Wade*, and legal elective abortions were not available. Her father made an appointment with an abortionist in Switzerland and prepared to fly her there for the procedure. The woman said she refused to go. Her father told her that if she did not go through with the abortion, she would never be welcome in his home again. The woman left home at seventeen, married her boyfriend and moved in with his family. They quickly moved to Arizona to save the family embarrassment and later gave birth to a healthy baby boy.

In the letter the woman explained how they struggled as a young couple trying to make ends meet, how she never finished high school and how they never went to college. After twelve years, the woman explained, the marriage ended in divorce. But she also explained that looking back, she would not trade any of it for the blessing of her son that God had given her. At the end of the letter the woman wrote, "Thank you, Adam, for being my 'gift from God.' There can be no greater gift than that of a child that God wants to be born . . . I love you, Mom" (Hamilton, 122-24).

Adam Hamilton is the pastor of the largest and fastest growing United Methodist Church in the United States. Consider the impact his leadership and ministry has had on his 13,000 member congregation. Imagine the lives that have been touched and transformed through the numerous books and Bible studies he has written. Adam Hamilton is just one small speck in God's creation, but a speck that was almost aborted; almost thrown in the trash heap; considered as the result of a shameful act, but saved by grace—saved by a mother's love for her unborn child.

Twenty-two years after *Roe v. Wade*, Norma McCorvey, better known as Jane Roe, found herself working in an abortion clinic. At that time, she was a heavy smoker and consumed alcohol like it was water. She did not like who she had become, not to mention the fact that she signed the document that allowed 35 million babies to be murdered. But what changed Norma's life, was a little girl named Emily who said, "I love you." How could anyone love someone who killed babies for a living? But little Emily did.

I am reminded of Jesus' words when he said, "Truly I tell you, unless you change and become like children, you will never enter the kingdom of heaven" (Matt. 18:3). Unless you change and become like Emily and love unconditionally, the kingdom of heaven cannot be experienced by you. And for the first time since her fight for *Roe v. Wade*, Norma no longer saw abortion as a convenient way of dealing with "products of conception" or "missed periods." Instead, abortion represented the "legal right" to end the life of a child as precious as Emily (McCorvey, *Won by Love*, 154). Through the life of one of God's "little ones" grace broke through the hardened heart. Shortly after her experience, Norma began the process of turning her life over to God. She went to church, confessed her sins, accepted Jesus Christ as her Lord and Savior and became a new creation. One who was responsible for many lives, received life. In 1997, Norma wrote a book about her experience titled, *Won By Love.*

Abortion is not about debating the topic of personhood and trying to decide if the child within has a right to live. Abortion is about recognizing God's grace in whatever form it presents itself; an unborn child or a redeemed sinner, and welcoming them both into the family of faith, the Church. Matthew 18:1-5 describes Jesus taking a child upon his lap and saying, "Whoever welcomes one such child in my name welcomes me."

CHAPTER SEVEN

Abortion, Complexity, and Grace

by Jayme Harvey

I grew up in a moderately conservative Christian community. Although I stood in solidarity with them on most of their theological, political, and philosophical convictions, I did not agree with their views surrounding abortion. As a young female, I found it difficult to encamp on the pro-life side of the issue solely because it was, and remains today, a predominately aged, male population that writes and passes our laws. Not adequately represented, I didn't feel it was right for the very male American government to tell me, a woman, what I could or could not do with my body. Today, I find myself leaning much more "liberally" on all of the big "issues," and also rethinking my stance on abortion, as contradictory as that might seem. The closer my husband and I are to starting our own family, the more I realize the deep and finalistic implications of abortion, implications I simply can't ignore. The issues surrounding abortion, are very complex. The deep and finalistic implications for the unborn child are just as deep and finalistic for his or her mother, whether she decides to abort or not.

My research on abortion revealed to me that it isn't a single issue at all. It isn't an easily decipherable issue that can be separated into good or evil, black or white, moral or immoral. Instead, abortion is centered in the middle of an inter-webbing of several different issues that surround and complicate it. Here, much more is at play than an individual woman deciding to "murder" her baby because she doesn't want it to mess up her life. Many people often want to simplify this complexity by dogmatically placing the heated issue in a neatly sealed pro-life or pro-choice box. When this happens, the rhetoric on both sides of the debate becomes so polarized that the issues that both fuel and complicate abortion cease to be addressed, such as the debate surrounding sexual education and providing birth control to students in public high schools, or the shame our society places on a premarital pregnancy. Out of fear that she will be disowned by her family and friends, a young woman makes the decision to end the life of her baby. Or what about the fact that there is little to no governmental funding for women who find themselves alone, pregnant, and poor? To simplify this issue into an absolute right or wrong is to add gasoline on an already blazing fire, perpetuating the cycle of violence that we enact upon one another, ourselves, and even on the cluster of cells which ultimately becomes a living and breathing creation. The question has been asked, "How should Christian leaders address the issue of abortion in our society today?" My answer to this question is with more grace, because many people find themselves on both sides of the debate. Abortion can't be sterilized into merely an argument; the lives of real people are at stake, both the women who find themselves in an impossible situation, and also the little hearts that beat inside of them. The unborn children and their mothers, whether they decide to abort or not, need to be loved and given more grace from church leaders and congregants alike, for the church, in many ways, has added to the number of abortions by casting shame and judgment, instead of love and compassion, on unwed mothers.

**Complexity**

Roger Paynter describes an unveiling of the complexity of this issue in his research. In a sermon on abortion to his congregation he says:

> If I have learned anything in these last few weeks of preparation, it is that there is simply "too much." There is so much to say, in fact, that I have a very, very hard time imagining how someone can investigate this issue and maintain even the slightest shred of arrogance about the "correctness" of his or her position. Yet people do maintain that, on both sides of the issue. I have a hard time understanding an attitude of complete confidence because abortion is just about the most extraordinarily complex medical, legal, philosophical, social, and moral issue I have investigated.[41]

---

[41] Roger Paynter, "Life in the Tragic Dimension: A Sermon on Abortion,"

How should Christian leaders respond to this complexity? Certainly not by asserting the absolute correctness of their position. After reading the heart wrenching stories on both sides of the debate, how can any one person have "complete confidence" in one's position? I believe that an "attitude of complete confidence" over one's position on the heated topic is not only arrogant, but it also polarizes the debate to the point where little is done about the "proliferation of abortions"[42] in our society today. Many pro-choice believers are not "pro-abortion"; they are concerned about the sheer amount of abortions each year. While this is true for persons on either side of the debate, it is especially significant for those encamped on the pro-life side. If they hold arrogantly to their position, it only perpetuates, or at the very least, does nothing to stop that which they hate the most, the death of unborn, growing children. Last week one of my "friends" on Facebook had a status that read, "Hitler–12 million, Stalin–20 million, *Roe vs. Wade*–50 million." My friend's oversimplification of the issue is highly problematic, and maybe even a detriment to his own cause. It certainly is not helpful.

Roger Paynter respects the complexity of this issue and calls for his listeners to respond with grace to all of those impacted by abortion. At the beginning of his sermon Paynter reveals the reason he decided to talk about such an intense debate:

> Oh, you haven't actually come out and called me foolish, but you have said, "Why ask for trouble? This is such a volatile issue; there is no way you can win." But, of course, "winning" isn't the issue when you bear the responsibility of standing behind the pulpit, or any pulpit, for that matter. The issue is to try to bring to bear the mercy and love and wisdom of the Gospel on the difficult realities of life . . . . I have known that the Gospel of Grace to which I am committed would not allow me forever to avoid this issue in a sermon.[43]

---

in Baird, *The Ethics of Abortion*, 232.
[42] Roger Paynter, 232.
[43] Ibid., 231.

His entire sermon cries out for grace, for the babies aborted, for their mothers, and for all of the women who find themselves in an impossible situation. Whether one agrees with Paynter's final position or not, his sermon exemplifies how Christian leaders should address the issue of abortion in our society today, with more grace for the very real people involved.

**Let's Call It What It Is**
Seeing is believing. Baby fetuses get mixed up with other debris and end up outside where everyday people have a chance to see their broken, unformed bodies. Richard Selzer writes, "There is no more. You turn to leave. Outside on the street, men are talking things over, reassuring each other that the right thing is being done. But just this once you know it isn't. You saw, and you know."[44] A medical student witnesses his first abortion in a university hospital:

> I know. We cannot feed the great numbers. There is no more room. I know, I know. It is a woman's right to refuse the risk, to decline the pain of childbirth. And an unwanted child is a very great burden. An unwanted child is a burden to himself. I know. And yet . . . there is the flick of the needle. I *saw* it. I *saw* . . . . I *felt*—in that room, a pace way, life prodded, life fending off. I saw life avulsed—swept by flood, blackening—then *out* . . . . It is a persona carried here as well as a person, I think. I think it is a signed piece, engraved with a hieroglyph of human genes. I did not think this until I saw. The flick. The fending off.[45]

For the people in these stories, seeing the reality of abortion had a profound effect. Their experience with abortion formed for them a belief about the issue. It wasn't out of a textbook, or a financially influenced political debate, by which they formed an opinion, but out of a very real, first person experience. For me, these two stories present a reality ,which I cannot ignore. The life that dwells inside of its mother is not just a cluster of cells. It is not just a fetus. It isn't just a life either. This little thing that wiggles and squirms and grows strong in its mother's womb is a

---

[44] Richard Selzer, "Abortion," in Baird, *The Ethics of Abortion*, 21.
[45] Richard Selzer, 23-24.

person that is loved and adored by God. It's very much a baby, no matter what week of gestation it is in, whether it looks like a clump of tissue, an alien with a misshaped head, or a fully formed infant with fingernails, hair, and eyelashes. And there is a tragic loss for God, for the mother, and for all of humanity when a baby is aborted. Let's call it what it is.

In an interesting twist, Naomi Wolf, a pro-choice feminist, calls for those standing on the side of pro-choice to a "radical shift in the pro-choice movement's rhetoric and consciousness about abortion." She writes:

> The movement's abandonment of what Americans have always, and rightly, demanded of their movements—an ethical core—and its reliance instead on a political rhetoric in which the fetus means nothing are proving fatal . . . . By refusing to look at abortion within a moral framework, we lose the millions of Americans who want to support abortion as a legal right but need to condemn it as a moral iniquity . . . . Clinging to a rhetoric about abortion in which there is no life and no death, we entangle our beliefs in a series of self-delusions, fibs and evasions. And we risk becoming precisely what our critics charge us with being: callous, selfish, and casually destructive men and women who share a cheapened view of human life.[46]

Naomi Wolf's comments exemplify what is lost when a person is arrogantly stuck in his or her position, refusing to look at or hear something different. To the detriment of the pro-choice movement, by refusing to examine abortion within a moral framework, it loses "the millions of Americans who want to support abortion as a legal right but need to condemn it as a moral iniquity." Although I don't believe abortion should be examined or considered just through the lens of moralism, nor does Naomi Wolf, her comments point to the possibility that women maintain the legal right to abort but fewer women actually enact that right, helping to decrease the "proliferation of abortions."[47] She goes on to write: "we need to be strong enough

---

[46] Naomi Wolf, "Our Bodies, Our Souls," in Baird, *The Ethics of Abortion*, 179-80.
[47] Roger Paynter, 232.

to acknowledge that this country's high rate of abortion—which ends more than a quarter of all pregnancies—can only be rightly understood as what Dr. Henry Foster was brave enough to call it: 'a failure.'"[48] The way in which we talk about this issue as Christian leaders has serious implications. In short, our rhetoric matters. If we call abortion murder, we demonize all of the women who felt there was no other choice but to end the life inside of them. Here, there is no grace for the women in the middle of very complex situations. If we call the little life inside of a woman merely a fetus or a cluster of cells, we deny the very real and finalistic implications of an abortion. We deny that a baby is lost. Neither of these extremes are helpful in reducing the "proliferation of abortions."[49] Instead, they both fuel the fire.

**Real People, Real Stories**
While taking the loss of a human life with utmost seriousness, Christian leaders must also take seriously the deep complexity of issues that push women to abort their babies. Often, much more is at play than an individual woman deciding to "murder" her baby because she doesn't want it to mess up her life. Anna Quindlen writes, "It is great mistake to believe that if abortion is illegal, it will be nonexistent . . . . Some kind of douche, some kind of drug, some kind of tubing: women will do it themselves. They always have. *They become so desperate for reasons we know nothing of, reasons not as easily quantifiable as being raped by a friend's father at age fourteen.*"[50] Anna Quindlen speaks of women who die from complications of performing their own abortion.[51] Clara Bell Duvall used a knitting needle for her abortion. She was 32 and a mother of five. She loved her children, and they loved her, but she was pregnant in the middle of the depression.[52] Quite possibly her panic over coming up with enough food for this baby, while continuing to semi-adequately feed the children she already had, drove her to puncturing her body with a tool for making clothes, which ultimately ended her life and the life of her baby. Anna Quindlen reminds us that

---

48 Naomi Wolf, 180.
49 Roger Paynter, 232.
50 Anna Quindlen, "The Abortion Orphans," in Baird, *The Ethics of Abortion*, 32.
51 Anna Quindlen, 32.
52 Ibid., 32-33.

women, whether illegal or not, will find ways to abort their babies. And it seems to me that she is saying that if abortion is illegal, stories like Clara's are only "the shadow of things to come."[53]

Frederica Mathewes-Green shares the stories of several women in a support group who had one or more abortions. Their stories are eye-opening and help me understand just a few of the circumstances that may lead a woman to have an abortion. Elizabeth's story sticks out to me the most.

> The thing I was fighting the most was a sense of shame, the image of people shaking their fingers at me—and some did! If I was going to continue the pregnancy, I would have had to have a support system: someone to tell me that I was a decent, good person, and that I would be taken care of. Nurturing Network has a whole wonderful program now, and I think if there had been something like that then, I would not have had the abortion.[54]

Society has done this to her. The church has done this to her. We play a more significant role in her abortion than we want to admit. First, we promise women a deep shaming for a pregnancy out of wedlock. Then, we leave them devalued with no monetary resources or emotional support. Here, we expect women to "make the right choice" after beating into them that they are horrible, sinful people. From a place of desperation we know nothing of she aborts the baby. And she is again shamed. The women who find themselves in the midst of an unwanted or unexpected pregnancy are real people with real stories. As Christian leaders, these women need the same amount of care, grace, and concern as do their unborn children. How should Christian leaders address the issue of abortion in our society today? By putting our judgmental fingers away, and offering the love, support, and grace these women need. I wonder how many other women like Elizabeth are out there? Those women who just needed someone to tell them that they are good and decent people who are loved by God. Maybe if the church puts their fingers away, remembering that we are not "any kind of absolute

---

[53] Ibid., 33.
[54] Frederica Mathewes-Green, *Real Choices,* 86.

moral judge,"[55] more women like Elizabeth would choose to not have the abortion.

**More Grace**

When I think about the women who find themselves in impossible situations, I think of Luke 7:36-50, where a sinful woman is forgiven. Like the woman in the story who "sins" not out of her own doing, but because of a larger societal system, women who abort their babies don't do so removed from society and other factors caught up in this heartbreaking issue. What follows is a short exegesis of Luke 7:36-50 to make my point clear, for it is reflective of the many women who cannot find a way out of their abortions, because of the world in which they live.

Luise Schottroff, a feminist theologian, says the text all but wants to say that this "sinful woman" is a prostitute.[56] Schottroff tackles the historical questions about what was going on in society when this passage was written, a long time ago in the Roman Empire. She answers the question, "Why does someone become a prostitute in the first place?" Why did *this* woman become a prostitute? She explains that women found themselves working as prostitutes mainly for economic reasons. Men were the breadwinners, and there were very few jobs that women were allowed to enter into in the first place. Often, those jobs didn't earn enough money to live on.[57] Widows and single women without fathers or brothers to "take care of them" didn't stand a good chance of being able to sustain themselves economically. These women didn't choose to be prostitutes because they wanted to. They didn't choose it at all. For many of them, prostitution was a necessity to survive, to eat. They were pushed into prostitution by the social system and then deemed as "unclean" or "sinful" by the very same system for being there.

Let's get back to our character. My guess is that she is quite beautiful, alluring and sensuous. Yet her beauty is assaulted by a societal system. She has been exploited. Instead of her beauty having the privilege of captivating her husband, it captivates many, because it has to. Her beauty is the source and sustenance of her life. It brings her bread. Because of what she does for a

---

55 Roger Paynter, 232.
56 Luise Schottroff, *Let the Oppressed Go Free*, 150.
57 Louise Schottroff, 150.

living . . . and maybe because of what has happened to her in the past, she doesn't get the honor of having a husband. She is disgraced, disgraced by a system that has placed her at the very bottom of the pecking order, condemned her for being there, and then kept her there with no practical way out. She can't just go get another job; there aren't any that will allow her to be self-supporting. So she finds herself at the Pharisee's house, holding an alabaster jar, waiting for Jesus.

Inside the house there is food spread over a large mat and guests are reclining on pillows. They are supporting themselves with their left arms and eating with their right hands, feet away from the mat and food.[58] Reclining among the guests is Jesus, but all eyes fall on the sinner when she walks into the room and approaches his feet. Curled over, she pulls out her hair pin and her dark Mediterranean curls flow swiftly down her back while her caramel cheeks blush at her action. As the salty tears from her eyes pour down her face and drip from her chin, the fat droplets find themselves washing the rough feet of Jesus. Like a towel, these beautiful curls begin to stick together at the ends where she is using them to dry the salty water from Jesus' feet. Between sobs, she presses her cold lips against his feet and anoints them with ointment. Unable to stop, she does this over and over again, kissing his feet and anointing them with oil. As she makes herself vulnerable, Jesus gracefully accepts this controversial gesture as one of love. I wonder how Jesus felt, watching and feeling a prostitute weep at his feet, while she washed them with her tears and dried them with her hair? He is perfectly aware of her predicament. He is aware of the system. He is aware, that even after she leaves this precious moment at his feet, she will have to go back and prostitute herself out for supper that evening, or the next. But still, the forgiveness he offers her covers over the entire span of time,[59] not just the moment they find themselves together. Notice that the passage makes no mention of Jesus saying, "Go and sin no more," like he does in other places of Scripture. Jesus does say, "Your faith has saved you; go in peace" (Luke 7:50). He knows it is not by choice that she "sins." He recognizes the assault on her beauty. He

---

[58] R. Allan Culpepper, "Luke." In *The New Interpreter's Bible: A Commentary in Twelve Volumes* (Nashville: Abingdon Press, 1997), 170.
[59] Louise Schottroff, 154.

might be the first person to recognize her true beauty, the kind that poured itself out as a love offering to the Redeemer, the one who can forgive all things.

Roger Paynter says to his congregation:

> These are all occurrences in a tragic and sinful world. Thus, abortion is not the automatic breaking of God's will. Neither can we glibly say that it is God's will that we perform abortion. In general, we should say that God is against the ending of all life, but that in some tragic circumstances, he understands—even allows—and certainly forgives the choices we have to make . . . . The tragic dimension of life is when there are no good choices left and everyone loses; when the choices left are not between good and evil, but between the lesser of two evils; or when we painfully, prayerfully, consider what is least bad.[60]

Much like I mourn the tragedy that the woman in Luke 7 has no choice but to go out and prostitute herself again so that she can eat, I mourn the tragedy that so many women are left with no good choices, and have to make a choice between "the lesser of the two evils." Here, everyone loses, the mother, the child, and a piece of our humanity. As Christian leaders we are to mourn and convey the depth of loss that is experienced in abortion, but we are also to be present, caring, and grace-filled for the women who find themselves having to make an impossible decision, no matter what they decide to do. Roger Paynter suggests: "if she feels guilt—offer and act out the Grace of God; if she feels grief—to offer and act out the Comfort of God; if she feels remorse—offer and act out the Peace of God; if she feels fear—to offer and act out the Love of God."[61]

---

[60] In Baird, *The Ethics of Abortion*, 236.
[61] In Baird, *The Ethics of Abortion*, 237.

CHAPTER EIGHT

Addressing the Issue of Abortion

by Joshua Hurd

There is, perhaps, not a more volatile topic one can raise than the subject of abortion. Both pro-life and pro-choice proponents have their respective reasons for believing the way they do. However, when they debate their positions in the public arena, they often talk past one another, as if they were speaking entirely different languages. Consequently, this failure to communicate, it seems, has stymied the possibility of all future conversation. As a result, each side has become satisfied with entrenching itself deeper and deeper within its own position, while at the same time satisfying itself with simple caricatures of fictional opponents. The purpose of this essay is to provide a new model for discussing and thinking about the topic of abortion. To meet this task, I will reflect on how the concept of dimensional anthropology[1] can help shed light on where much of the confusion seems to stem.

In his book *The Trinitarian Self: The Key to the Puzzle of Violence,* Charles Bellinger asserts that there is a discernible structure to human existence.[2] Human existence, he asserts, is tripartite or consists of three dimensions. These three dimensions include: "the vertical axis of God and nature, the horizontal plane of social existence, and the temporal trajectory of individual selfhood."[3] Consequently, these three dimensions will provide an outline for our discussion of abortion.

---

[1] Charles K. Bellinger, *The Trinitarian Self: The Key to the Puzzle of Violence* (Eugene, OR: Pickwick Publications, 2008).
[2] Ibid, xi.
[3] Ibid.

**Temporal Trajectory of Individual Selfhood**
We begin our discussion from the perspective of the individual self, as one who is moving forward through time. I start with this dimension first, because much of the abortion debate centers on individual rights. The pro-choice side focuses upon the individual rights of the mother; the pro-life side focuses upon the individual rights of the unborn. Thus, both sides will often share a common rhetoric in this regard. In her widely anthologized essay "A Defense of Abortion," Judith Jarvis Thomson states, "I propose, then, that we grant that the fetus is a person from the moment of conception."[4] While Thomson is willing to grant the premise that the fetus is a person from the very moment of conception, she does not think that it necessarily follows that abortion should be prohibited based on this assertion. In fact, Thomson wants to contest the claim that "Every person has a right to life. So the fetus has a right to life."[5] However, she bases her argument on the rights of the mother. In her mind, the mother's rights over her own body trump the rights of the unborn.

Now this may seem like a strange line of strategy to follow. How could someone grant that a fetus is, in fact, a person, and then proceed to argue that abortion is still a legitimate practice? For many of us, including myself, this appears to be a horrific proposition. Yet Thomson appears to be fully convinced of her position. When viewed from the perspective of dimensional anthropology, the basis of Thomson's argument soon becomes apparent. Thomson builds her argument significantly, if not entirely, from the sole perspective of individual selfhood. It is for this reason, then, that Thomson can carry out such a radical proposal. Her interest is to protect the *individual's* rights at all costs. What is strange, however, is that Thomson carries out her argument to such an extent that she seeks to protect individual rights against the intrusive rights of the other, i.e. the unborn child. This is demonstrated by her fictitious analogy of the violinist who suffers from a kidney ailment, so they kidnapped another person in order to use that person's kidneys as a filter for the violinist's.[6] Another illustration which Thomson gives is the

---

[4] Judith Jarvis Thomson, "A Defense of Abortion" in Baird, *The Ethics of Abortion,* 242.
[5] Ibid.
[6] Ibid.

woman who is trapped in a house with a perpetually growing child.[7] In both of these stories, the woman represents the victim, the one who is under attack, and the unborn child represents the victimizer, the one who is doing the attacking. Later, Thomson expounds upon what she has been arguing throughout her essay:

> But I would stress that I am not arguing that people do not have a right to life—quite to the contrary, it seems to me that the primary control we must place on the acceptability of an account of rights is that it should turn out in that account to be a truth that all persons have a right to life. I am arguing only that having a right to life does not guarantee having either a right to be given the use of or a right to be allowed continued use of another person's body—even if one needs it for life itself. So the right to life will not serve the opponents of abortion in the very simple and clear way in which they seem to have thought it would.[8]

At this time one may wonder: At what point does the child's rights become his or her *own* protected rights? Thomson suggests that this occurs when the parents have taken the child home with them, "then they have assumed responsibility for it, they have given it rights, and they cannot now withdraw support from it at the cost of its life because they now find it difficult to go on providing for it."[9] At no point before this *granting of rights,* however, do the parents have any obligatory commitment to the child. In her own words, "they do not simply by virtue of their biological relationship to the child who comes into existence have a special responsibility for it."[10]

How might a person address Thomson's position from a more complex, dimensional anthropology? As it has already been demonstrated, Thomson's position is a very lopsided approach to the abortion topic. In fact, Thomson's position almost completely resides within the confines of the individual self. Now one may grant that Thomson does show a degree of consistency in her argument, emphasizing the mother's rights over her own body at

---

[7] Ibid, 244-245.
[8] Ibid, 248.
[9] Ibid, 254.
[10] Ibid.

all costs. However, Thomson does seem to curb her position a bit towards the end, when the situation turns into "the set of parents."[11] Why does Thomson now, all of the sudden, decide to include someone else in the scenario? In all the previous illustrations, it is the woman alone who faces the threat of the child. It seems that Thomson has realized that, at some point, one has to connect the autonomous individual with the rest of society. In dimensional anthropology, this is called the horizontal plane; it represents the social aspect of human existence. Human beings do not live within vacuums; thus, the horizontal plane addresses this dimension.

**The Vertical Axis**
What about the third aspect of dimensional anthropology, the vertical axis? Thomson does not seem to give much thought to how God might factor into the equation. In fact, Thomson essentially takes Jesus' parable of the Good Samaritan and turns it on its head. Her position is that while it might be a noble act of the woman to carry the child, the woman in under no obligation to do so. On the lower part of the vertical axis, i.e. nature, Thomson too shows little concern. If one includes the biological piece of human existence under the domain of nature, then Thomson does not appear to show any vested interests. Although, I am basing this assessment predominantly on Thomson's stating, "they [the parents] do not simply by virtue of their biological relationship to the child who comes into existence have a special responsibility for it."[12] This seems odd, since all human beings come into existence through biological dependency on their parents. However, Thomson is focusing only upon the dimension of individual selfhood in human existence.

In his essay "Nature as Demonic in Thomson's Defense of Abortion," John T. Wilcox argues that Thomson's argument is based upon a particular, mythological understanding of metaphysics.[13] Wilcox expresses his concern in a comical statement: "In ordinary pregnancy, you and your partners are the only ones responsible; you and he have done voluntarily what got you pregnant. There is no burglar, no rights-violator, on the

---

[11] Ibid, 254.
[12] Ibid, 254.
[13] In Baird, *The Ethics of Abortion,* 257.

scene—unless we imagine that *nature* is the violator. 'Here we were, minding our own business, having intercourse—when nature got me pregnant."[14] He continues, "To fill out this story of Thomson's, to make the typical pregnancy analogous to burglary, *we have to introduce some unjust force* analogous to the burglar; nature, perhaps—nature as demonic, out to get you, violating your rights as you innocently go about your business."[15] Although Wilcox is clearly poking fun at Thomson, he, nevertheless, is raising legitimate concerns. From the perspective of individual selfhood, Thomson identifies the enemy as coming from the vertical axis. What is interesting, however, is that Thomson does not blame God, which would point toward the upper part of the vertical axis. Instead, Thomson identifies the enemy as being nature itself.

**The Horizontal Plane**
We now move our discussion from the perspective of the individual selfhood to the horizontal plane. This dimension, as we previously noted, pertains to the social aspect of human existence. From this perspective, the abortion debate is framed not as an individual issue of personal rights, but as a social issue. In her essay, "Abortion as a Sacrament: Mimetic Desire and Sacrifice in Sexual Politics," Bernadette Waterman Ward incorporates the thought of René Girard in order to address the topic of abortion.[16] Ward too discusses the self, but under different terms. In agreement with Girard, Ward understands human beings as being essentially social creatures. She states, "From the nursery we are each other's disciples, wanting each other's toys not because of their inherent virtue so much as because someone else has seen some virtue in them."[17]

Ward is describing here what Girard calls mimetic desire. According to Girard's theory, human beings do not possess their own innate desires as such. Rather, human beings receive their desires by imitating particular models. Furthermore, mimetic desire is not bad in and of itself. For instance, there are good models which are worthy of imitation, e.g. Jesus. However, when people choose bad models this creates a sort of rivalry between

---

[14] Ibid, 263.
[15] Ibid.
[16] In *Contagion: Journal of Violence, Mimesis, and Culture,* 7: 18-35.
[17] Ibid, 19.

them; individuals come into competition with one another, for they are all after everyone else's desires. This escalating rivalry often ends in violence. Furthermore, this escalating violence can get to the point where everyone is against everyone else. In order to avoid utter chaos, Girard asserts, societies focus their attention upon a single individual or a small group of people. Consequently, this small minority is then accused as being the cause of the community's problems. This has a unifying effect for the community, as they come together against the one or the few. Furthermore, this process of *letting off some steam* is what Girard has termed "scapegoating."

Now that we are more familiar with Girard's basic theory, how does Bernadette Ward enlist Girard's thought in order to address the issue of abortion? She writes, "The process of instability leading to sacrificial crisis, which Girard describes in many works, can be seen clearly in the development of American abortion culture."[18] What Bernadette Ward posits, then, is that the intensification of mimetic desire has created rivalry between women and men on many different fronts. Furthermore, there is a tendency for women to receive the greater impact of these effects. For example, describing the "familial breakdown" in American society, Ward states: "Parenthood virtually imposes on a divorced woman both financial insecurity and undesirability as a mate. As the incidence of divorce rose sharply, American women lost the protections offered by male obligation to marriage partners."[19]

One can see, then, from the perspective of dimensional anthropology, Ward's essay focuses primarily upon the horizontal plane. In other words, one views abortion as being the result of injustices within social structures. One example of social injustice, Ward cites, is the discrimination of women in the workplace. Since the norm for American culture is the "non-childbearing" male, pregnant women or women with children do not stand much of a chance in the job market.[20] Left in this dire situation, Ward suggests, "A woman faced with economic and social oppression connected to the normal functioning of her body has two obvious choices: she can reject the definitions of her entire political world and try to set up some sort of

---

[18] Ibid, 22.
[19] Ibid.
[20] Ibid, 23.

rebellion—or she can conclude that the enemy is within; is indeed her own pregnant body and the fetus growing there."[21] This statement highlights the difference between Ward's position and that of Thomson. While Thomson predominantly addresses abortion from the rights of the woman, even though there might not be any circumstantial pressures, Ward's position focuses on societal influences. She states, "Most mothers who actually abort do so because they feel they have no free choice. They are under a terrible compulsion, and the compulsion is not physical."[22] Note the difference in rhetoric between Ward's and Thomson's position.

Facing their options, women often choose abortion over the option of suffering at the hands of societal injustices. In this way, they too are venting their violence onto someone else. As Ward states, "abortion in America precisely fits the structure of religious sacrifice, where the best victims are the most defenseless."[23] The end result is that fetuses become America's scapegoats.

As it has been briefly sketched out in this essay, the abortion debate is plagued with either lopsided arguments or missing elements. It is easy to buttress one's own position by caricaturing one's opponent. However, I think a complex dimensional anthropology forces us to challenge our own assumptions. By this means, there is hope for future dialogue on this most important problem.

---

[21] Ibid.

[22] Ibid, 26

[23] Ibid, 23. Ward also states that, "Like a classic sacrificial victim, the fetus is both blamed for the disorder surrounding its conception and acknowledged as innocent, sometimes at the same time.

CHAPTER NINE

A Perspective on Abortion: Science and Theology in the Balance

by Rashona Thomas

Reconciling my theological beliefs with those that have come from my formal scientific training has been an interesting and ongoing task. While theology and science seem to complement each other at times and at other times contradict one another, I believe that both offer valuable truths each within its own arena. Neither theology nor science can completely explain or justify the other. Although at different stages of my life I have considered my position on the abortion issue, I am now approaching the task again. I am analyzing and weighing in the balance my understandings of science and theology and evaluating how they frame the production of my public theology and what position I believe Christian leaders should hold on the issue of abortion.

Theologically I hold that there is life at conception. Paul Simmons suggests that some who are anti-abortion because of religious reasons turn to scriptures such as Jeremiah 1:5 and Psalm 139:13-15 to support their claim.[1] While I do believe such scriptures inform us of truths about God, I do not believe, when considered in context, they can be rightly used to solidify the argument that abortion is wrong. Such scriptures inform us that God is an exquisite Creator who values life. God, as the Creator of life, knows the fullness of potentiality of even fetal life that we can completely disregard at worst, and only wonderfully imagine at best. As the Creator, God set into motion a cycle of life and development, the mysteries of which human beings are continually learning. For all of this we should praise God and refine our perceptions of life such that we highly regard it.

---

[1] Paul D. Simmons. "Personhood, the Bible, and Abortion," in Baird, *The Ethics of Abortion*, 210-14.

The biological perspective that life actually begins *before* conception because both sperm and egg are living prior to it is a valid one. This observation points to the problem in the pro-choice stance that denies that a fetus is a living being. It is counterintuitive that the joining of two living entities could result in anything else but another living entity. Even if one agrees that both sperm and egg are living prior to conception, it does not solidify the *identity* of the resultant being. I hold that at conception there exists a living being that is of the human species, yet this does not altogether answer the question of personhood. Is the living being a person?

Paul Simmons offers a biblical view of personhood based on three biblical texts: Genesis 1:26-28, 2:7, and 3:22. He argues that these texts support first that persons breathe. Next, that persons are like God in having self-awareness, the ability to be introspective and retrospective, and to discern God's activity in their lives. Lastly he argues that persons are moral decision makers. "The biblical portrait of person, therefore, is that of a complex, many-sided creature with godlike abilities and the moral responsibility to make choices."[2] For Simmons, because a fetus does not meet these criteria, it is not considered a person.

Mary Anne Warren sets forth five characteristics as central to personhood: consciousness, the ability to reason, self-motivated activity, communication capacity, and self-awareness. While she offers nebulous commitments concerning how many or what combination of these five characteristics are necessary to declare what is personhood, she more definitively asserts what is not personhood. "All we need to claim, to demonstrate that a fetus is not a person is that any being which satisfies *none* of [these five characteristics] is certainly not a person."[3]

A problem with these arguments is they leave room to conclude that newborns, infants, premature babies, and even people with mental handicaps are not persons. Newborn babies do not have the ability to be introspective or discern God's activity in their lives, and frankly some forty year old adults cannot yet discern God's activity in their lives. Additionally, according to Warren's criteria it is possible for an individual to be a person one moment and not a person the next such as in the

---

[2] Ibid., 210.
[3] Mary Anne Warren, "On the Moral and Legal Status of Abortion," in Baird, *The Ethics of Abortion*, 274-75.

cases of accidents that result in traumatic brain injury or comatose states. Such individuals are not always conscious or self-aware with the capacity to reason or communicate, or perform any self-motivated activity. It is clear that attempts to use such rigid criteria to define personhood, whether based on scripture or science, are problematic. They have the potential to expose the absurdity of disregarding the personhood of individuals such as newborn infants and the physically or mentally debilitated.

I do not believe personhood can be attributed to an embryo, although it is a living being and of human substance. "That many people believe that a zygote is a person does not alter the fact that the attribution of personhood to a zygote is based on metaphysical speculation, not scientific fact."[4] I do not know that anyone could clearly demarcate when personhood begins without major flaws in the theory. Personhood is most easily captured for me with a fluid combination of biological and physical characteristics. I find value in the notion of viability or the Catholic understanding of quickening as indicators of personhood. I also find value in certain physical traits that when seen, an individual can recognize features they have in common with the fetus, like general body structure, organs, and external genitalia. In this way, there is a certain psychological connection that can be made (and not easily denied) by the observer that what they are observing looks very much like themselves, albeit smaller and less developed.

It is not critical to my theology to recognize a zygote as a person. I try to hold theology and science in tension without the need for one to trump the other. The amazement and miracle of pregnancy and fetal development is that if given time, the zygote will grow and change until the baby that is born does not at all resemble the zygote it used to be. This process is no less miraculous and the creative brilliance of God is not minimized at all if the zygote is not recognized as a person. It is no less miraculous if I do not acknowledge that the "hand of God" is at all times intricately involved with shaping every detail of the human body *in utero*. The value and divine miracle in pregnancy is captured throughout the entire process by which, because of

---

4 Paul D. Simmons. "Religious Liberty and Abortion Policy Casey as Catch-22," in Baird, *The Ethics of Abortion*, 158.

fascinating biology created by God, embryonic life develops into an undeniable person.

Central to the abortion debate is a woman's right to choose and control her own body. I agree that an individual should have autonomy over one's own body, however, when one's body is being shared by another living being, by no choice of that living being, the notion of autonomy must take on different dimensions. "Autonomy and relationality are . . . inseparable . . . . Choices about exercising our freedom should infuse, enhance, or maintain respect in our relationships with one another."[5] A pregnant woman is in the most intimate of relationships with another (the fetus). This relationship is difficult to deny. Consequently, a woman's choices are no longer merely *her* choices. By this I do not mean that her choices are someone else's. I mean her choices are informed by a particular context (pregnancy) and she now must consider how this context is impacting and shaping the decision she believes is her autonomous one. She must consider how her context is shaping her beliefs about the choices available to her in the present, her vision of the future and how her decisions will affect "the other" that shares her context. "A woman, involuntarily pregnant, has a moral obligation to the now-existing dependent fetus . . . . The woman's obligation arises both from her status as a human being embedded in the interdependent human community and her unique lifegiving female reproductive power."[6]

Many years ago during my residency at a prominent medical center in the Dallas-Fort Worth metroplex, I spent time in the area of organ transplantation. I will never forget attending a meeting in which a transplant board reviewed candidate files to decide who would receive a much needed organ and who would not. The case discussions considered everything from the candidate's race, gender, age, and health status to social status, career, and social habits. It was quite unsettling to listen to a discussion that hinged on projections of which candidate might potentially experience a long and flourishing life subsequent to the transplant and which had the most potential to contribute to the world. It was clear to me that a sixty year old, blue collar worker may not have been considered in the same light as a

---

[5] Traci C. West, *Disruptive Christian Ethics*, 63.
[6] Sidney Callahan, "Abortion and the Sexual Agenda," in Baird, *The Ethics of Abortion*, 171.

college-educated, young woman with two school-aged children. Once each decision was made, a huge red "DENIED" stamp was placed on the files of those who would not receive a transplant. This same red stamp was indelibly placed on my mind. I watched the file stamped "DENIED" slide along the table and quickly understood that intrinsically as a society we do not place equal moral value or extend equal moral rights to everyone.

What rights does a fetus have? If it has rights, what or who grants it those rights? How do the rights of a fetus stand against the rights of the one carrying it? My belief on rights revolves around the notion that the fetus is alive as understood by the process set in motion by a creative God and scientifically evidenced by cell multiplication, growth and intricate developmental changes. It is a living being. Because God values the life of the unborn, we should not devalue it. I cannot argue though that the unborn have the *same* rights as other individuals, especially considering that adults within society are not extended equal moral rights as evidenced in part by considerations of the transplant board. To think that the unborn do have the same rights would imply that "justice requires that those who abort them for reasons less than self-defense must be recognized as full-fledged murderers and treated as such."[7] I think this is both unreasonable and impractical as trying to justly implement such a practice would undoubtedly lead to circular arguments of what constitutes self-defense and what kind of murder charge and punishment would be fitting.

Despite the inequity in fundamental moral rights between parents-to-be and the fetus, I believe that the fetus has "the right not to be killed without *very* good reason."[8] Just because adults have different moral rights than a fetus does not mean they have the right to deny that the unborn has *any* rights at all. Don Marquis says: "What primarily makes killing wrong is . . . its effect on the victim. The loss of one's life is one of the greatest losses one can suffer. The loss of one's life deprives one of all the experiences, activities, projects, and enjoyments that would otherwise have constituted one's future."[9] A fetus has the right to

---

[7] Joan C. Callahan, "The Fetus and Fundamental Rights," in Baird, *The Ethics of Abortion*, 305.

[8] Ibid., 297-298.

[9] Don Marquis, "Why Abortion is Immoral," in Baird, *The Ethics of Abortion*, 315.

not have its developmental processes aborted out of convenience to the one carrying it. The unborn should have the right to experience the fullness of life simply because they are living beings and God values them.

A woman can easily overpower this right, as in most abortion cases, but then again the rights of the powerless, the poor and the voiceless of society can always be overpowered by those positioned in places of power relative to them. While a pregnant 17 year old woman may in many ways be powerless by society's terms, she does hold a position of power relative to the fetus. Power is always relative. The desires of those with power can easily overshadow those without it as a matter of common practice, but this does not mean that the rights of the powerless and voiceless do not exist. The same is true for the right of a fetus to not be aborted only this right cannot be upheld or defended by the voiceless fetus itself. Someone else in a position of relative power must speak on its behalf.

Given that abortion deprives a fetus of the opportunity to experience fullness of life, abortion should not be used merely to avoid perceived inconveniences of pregnancy or parenthood. It should not be used as an antidote for sexual irresponsibility. "Fifty-seven percent of unintended pregnancies come about because the parents used no contraception at all."[10] Some argue that a woman terminating an unintended pregnancy that she is not ready for is an act of sexual responsibility. For me, abortion does not demonstrate sexual responsibility given sexual responsibility is best demonstrated proactively, not reactively. There are simply too many highly effective contraceptive options readily available for both men and women to not use them. Bypassing these readily available options is no less than self-centered and irresponsible.

Human beings have an innate inclination toward self; self-preservation, self-gratification, self-interests, etc. At the root of the majority of abortions is self-centeredness, whether it is the woman whose education will be disrupted by a pregnancy, the family members who are concerned with how the family name will be smeared because of a pregnancy, or the man who does not want the responsibility of emotionally or financially supporting the mother or child. Self-centeredness is at the root.

---

[10] Naomi Wolf, "Our Bodies, Our Souls," in Baird, *The Ethics of Abortion*, 185.

In much rarer cases abortions are chosen out of concern for "the other," the baby that will be born. In rare cases abortions are chosen to prevent the innocent young life from experiencing physical hardship or pain that will certainly come with a debilitating genetic defect or disease that will result in inevitable and early death for the child. These endpoints are not consistent with a life of fullness or flourishing. In such cases when the difficult choice to terminate a pregnancy is chosen, I consider a love of life to still be present. A parent-to-be has taken all into consideration and loves the unborn enough to deny themselves a child and not permit such terrible realities to be experienced or endured by the child that would be born.

While the church in America has done well at taking a stance for or against the issue of abortion, it has not done well at being committed to demonstrating love through pragmatic support of the women who make the decisions either for or against. If we, as church leaders, choose to lift up the value of life of the unborn, we must also be willing to provide essential emotional support to the woman who chooses to endure the emotional turbulence of giving her child up for adoption and that which may subsequently come from strained relationships. If we choose to uphold the value of unborn life, we must also be willing to bridge the gap and provide practical means of economic support and direction for women who choose to keep their children despite the economic hardships they may face as a result. To acknowledge and remember the value of unborn life, we must be willing to embrace, not demean women who saw no feasible alternatives and chose abortions. We do not have to agree with their decision, but it is incongruent to say we value one life while we demean another. Lastly, if the church chooses to uphold the value of unborn life, we must be willing to come out of the delusion and denial regarding sex and sexuality. We must be willing to openly discuss these issues *in the church*, both retrospectively, such as in support groups for adults who have faced the decision of abortion, and prospectively such as within youth ministries where young people can more fully understand the complexity and gravity of the consequences of their sexual choices.

In conclusion, I believe Christian leaders should be advocates for the life of the unborn. We should be willing to hold together the theological and scientific aspects of the abortion issue without *necessarily* forcing science to submit to our theological beliefs. We must acknowledge the frailties and deficits in social, economic, and relational support that many young women face which often inform their decisions to have abortions, and be prepared and willing to bridge these gaps. As Christian leaders, we must remain cognizant of the fact that it is easy to merely dehumanize and demean others and become completely blind to our own hypocrisy. We, as the church, are not called to dehumanize our neighbor but to love our neighbor. Such love includes being willing to make sure alternatives to abortion have been clearly presented and being willing to offer the necessary emotional and psychological support if a young woman chooses the alternative *and* extend the same support if she chooses to terminate the pregnancy. We should not shrink back from articulating our convictions, but in doing so we must with all humility demonstrate the love of God and love of life to all, including those who choose differently than us.

CHAPTER TEN

Which of Your Neighbors is More Like Hitler?:
An Analysis of the Analogy of Abortion and Genocide

by Justin Tiemeyer

Do the members of the Supreme court murder babies? Is Planned Parenthood a place at which genocide is practiced? Are the unborn lower beings? Do the citizens of the United States of America actively facilitate genocide whereas the citizens of Germany during the Holocaust were mostly passive? Is the United States one giant Auschwitz? Are companies who manufacture devices and medicines used in abortion responsible for mass execution?

At the beginning of the chapter titled "If Hitler Were Alive, Whose Side Would He Be On?" in Gloria Steinem's book *Outrageous Acts and Everyday Rebellions*, there is a series of quotations used by anti-abortionists that imply that the answer to all of these questions is yes.[1] These slogans are only a few of the rhetorical situations in which abortion is compared either to the Holocaust, black slavery or infanticide in particular or to genocide in general. If you, upon reading the questions above, answered "no" to any of the questions in the above paragraph then there is reason for you to question the use of this analogy when it comes to the rhetoric of the abortion debate. It is my intention in this paper to analyze a variety of individuals and groups involved in the discussion of whether or not the analogy of abortion and genocide is legitimate rhetoric as well as to provide an analysis of the rhetoric itself, its strengths and its shortcomings.

---

[1] Gloria Steinem, *Outrageous Acts and Everyday Rebellions*, 305-06.

## History of the Abortion as Genocide Analogy

Regarding the rhetoric concerned with the comparison between abortion in the United States of America and acts of genocide including, but not limited to, the European Holocaust and slavery in the United States of America, there are three stages of rhetoric that I would like to address. The first stage is that of the individuals who believe that there are many connections to be drawn between abortion practices in the United States of America and historical acts of genocide. I call this the *abortion is genocide* stage, and note that most participants in this stage of rhetoric are specifically focused on the comparison of abortion with the Holocaust. The second stage is that of the individuals who believe that the connections between abortion practices and genocide are at the very least incorrect and at most repugnant. I call this the *abortion is not genocide* stage of rhetoric, and note that those who fit into this category are mostly reacting to those in the first stage of rhetoric. Finally, there is a third stage in which the assertion that *abortion is genocide* is recognized (stage one) but from the perspective of criticizing the arguments of those who believe that *abortion is not genocide* (stage two). I call this the *abortion is totally genocide* stage, and note that those who fit into this stage are reacting to those in the second category who are reacting to the first stage.

Perhaps the loudest voice in the *abortion is genocide* stage is that of Greg Cunningham and the Center for Bio-Ethical Reform (CBR), whose Genocidal Awareness Project (GAP) visits college campuses with pictures of the Holocaust, black lynching, and other victims of genocide juxtaposed opposite aborted fetuses.[2] Other voices include Jewish rabbi Jacob Neusner,[3] Patrick Riley, Raymond J. Adamek, Congressman Robert K. Dornan, Professor William C. Brennan, and anti-abortion newsletter *The Abolitionist*,[4] as well as various Catholics,[5] individuals at the 1979 Right-to-Life Convention,[6] and leaders and members of Christian churches.[7] While most of this rhetoric appears as

---

[2] Joyce Arthur, "No, Virginia, Abortion Is NOT Genocide," *The Humanist* 60, no. 4 (July/August 2000), 20.

[3] Jacob Neusner, "Israel's Holocaust," *Human Life Review* 25, no. 2 (Spring 1999), 102.

[4] Gloria Steinem, *Outrageous Acts and Everyday Rebellions*, 305-306.

[5] Cathleen Kaveny, "A Flawed Analogy: Prochoice Politicians & The Third Reich," *Commonweal* 135, no. 12 (June 20, 2008), 6.

[6] Gloria Steinem, 305.

emotionally charged propaganda, this stage is not without its calm and careful scholars. Most notable of these scholars is James T. Burtchaell who writes in his book *Rachel Weeping: The Case Against Abortion* that abortion is similar not only to the Holocaust and American slavery, but also to historical practices of infanticide, insofar as victims are depersonalized, the acts are disguised in euphemism and those who commit the acts deny responsibility.[8]

In the *abortion is not genocide* stage, many have lined up in order to specifically address the inadequacy and insulting nature of such an analogy. Cathleen Kaveny, author of "A Flawed Analogy: Prochoice Politicians & The Third Reich," Robert McAfee Brown, author of "Abortion and the Holocaust," and Robert G. Weisbord, author of "Legalized Abortion and the Holocaust: An Insulting Parallel" belong in this camp. John Hunt also places the National Abortion and Reproductive Rights Action League (NARAL), founders Betty Friedan, Lawrence Lader, Bernard Nathanson, feminist Gloria Steinem, and syndicated columnist Ellen Goodman in this category.[9] Another that I would include in this stage is Joyce Arthur, who I have set apart because of her use of the concept of absurdity in the face of the *abortion is genocide* stage. In "No, Virginia, Abortion Is NOT Genocide," she hypothesizes that "most people can't be bothered to refute something so obviously preposterous and don't wish to dignify it with a reply."[10] While many of this second stage are engaged in seriously considering the juxtaposition posed by those of the first stage, it is interesting to note that there are people like Arthur who force the reader to consider whether or not absurdity, humor, or sarcasm are valid methods of criticism.

The final stage which I have called *abortion is totally genocide* is perhaps the least popular. The most important scholar I have come across in this category is John Hunt, the author of "Abortion and Nazism: Is There Really a Connection?" An interesting discussion topic that could be brought up is the

---

[7] Robert McAfee Brown, "Abortion and the Holocaust," *Christian Century* 101, no. 33 (October 31, 1984), 1004.

[8] Lisa Sowle Cahill, review of *Rachel Weeping*, by James T. Burtchaell. *Journal of Law and Religion* 1, no. 1 (1983): 252.

[9] John Hunt, "Abortion and Nazism: Is There Really A Connection?" In *Life and Learning VI*, Joseph Koterski, ed., 325-326.

[10] Joyce Arthur, "No, Virginia, Abortion Is NOT Genocide," 21.

question of why there are so few people responding critically to the critical analysis of abortion and genocide propaganda. Joyce Arthur suggests that individuals interested in propagating the analogy of abortion and genocide are less interested in discussion than they are in inciting anger, distress and trauma.[11]

## Rhetorical Analysis of the Abortion as Genocide Analogy

An analysis of the analogy of abortion and genocide is anything but simple. The terms compared by Cathleen Kaveny alone include "prochoice politicians" and "the Third Reich," "politicians who support abortion rights" and "Nazis," "Catholics who would vote for such politicians" and "citizens of the Third Reich who were indifferent to the plight of those condemned to the gas chamber," "the American prochoice legal regime" and "Nazi Germany," "the American practice of legalized abortion" and "the Holocaust," "the treatment of the unborn under U.S. law" and "Nazi German's treatment of the Jews," "legalized abortion [not necessarily American, as above]" and "the Holocaust," and "women and their unborn children" and "Nazis and Jews." Cathleen Kaveny is not an author who I would describe as unorganized or "all over the place," and yet I counted eight separate and different (sometimes subtly so) comparisons in her article. The rhetoric used by all three stages of this debate includes far more different comparisons than the eight found in Kaveny, and the difference between these distinct analogies can make a world of difference. Consider a simple comparison like "the practice of abortion in the United States of America" and "the Holocaust." Here we are comparing an historical occurrence with another historical occurrence, the proper noun Holocaust, which is synonymous with the Hebrew designation Shoah, representing the European execution of millions of Jews. Now consider a simple comparison like "abortion" and "holocaust." Here we are comparing two generic ideas or practices, the common noun holocaust, which derives from the Greek words *holos*, or "whole," and *kaustos*, or "burnt," representing any of a number of situations in which something is burned in its entirety. A mere substitution of "abortion" for "the practice of abortion in the United States of America" or of "the Holocaust" for "holocaust" can change ones rhetoric entirely, and yet the

---

[11] Joyce Arthur, "No, Virginia, Abortion Is NOT Genocide," 20.

debate surrounding this analogy quickly conflates a wide variety of terminology, substituting one for another as it supports one's arguments.

Another important thing to think about in the analysis of rhetoric is the simple question of what rhetoric is understood as, what forms of rhetoric are accepted in discussion, and how rhetoric is judged as good or bad. The Aristotelian rhetoric that is taught in English and philosophy courses across the nation values an appeal to logic or *logos*, but this does not necessitate that all rhetoric must be logical, for example. Balanced by *pathos* and *ethos*, it is very probable that rhetoric can exist with little or no connection to logic, especially if it appeals to one's feelings or ethical sense. Ancient teachers of rhetoric known as Sophists were known for purposely confounding logic by tracing illegitimate connections between words that vaguely resemble one another, causing many to call such misleading rhetoric "sophistry." It would seem that anything can count as rhetoric insofar as it attempts to convince an audience of something, and that rhetoric is judged not by its ethical content (remember that *ethos* is merely one dimension of rhetoric) but by its ability to convince. As such, one could suggest that each of these different forms of rhetoric certainly has historically convinced audiences of its worth or veracity and can be determined good rhetoric as a result. Of course, to leave it at that would, I think, be irresponsible.

As a result of the argument regarding the conflation of comparisons, I think it wise to consider a couple of different arguments regarding the comparison between abortion and genocide more closely. In the Jacob Neusner article, "Israel's Holocaust," Neusner reacts emotionally to the issue of abortion in Israel. He does nothing to conceal this act and he does not feel that he should conceal this act. Speaking as a Jewish rabbi he understands (or, at least, ought to understand) that when he speaks his opinion or argument will be received as a theologically informed opinion or a theological argument. As a matter of fact, it could be argued that this article resembles, in many ways, the lamentation format of writing from Hebrew scripture. The first sentence of his work is, "My heart is broken."[12] He expresses a legitimate feeling toward hearing that a baby has been aborted in

---

[12] Jacob Neusner, "Israel's Holocaust," 102.

the same way that broken-heartedness can be seen as a legitimate feeling toward any kind of death. His second paragraph begins by saying, "No law stood in the way of this act, no argument from morality. The Torah did not intervene."[13] In this sentence he expresses a sense of righteous indignation toward the state of affairs in which the unborn are killed without intervention. He compares *the feeling* of reflecting upon the lives lost in the Holocaust with *the feeling* of reflecting upon the lives lost due to legalization of abortion in Israel. As such, I have no critique for Jacob Neusner. That these two feelings are close in his heart and that he wishes to speak to others and convince them to recognize this feeling is in no way misleading, illogical or wrong.

Consider also the arguments of James T. Burtchaell in his book *Rachel Weeping*. Burtchaell makes a series of valid points regarding the comparisons not just of abortion and the Holocaust, but of abortion and black slavery, and abortion and infanticide. He points to serious points in which the analogy is correct, as Lisa Sowle Cahill so succinctly summarizes, such as depersonalization, misleading rhetoric and the denial of responsibility.[14] The rhetorical problem with James T. Burtchaell's analogy (as well as in the analogies of many others, and perhaps with the concept of analogy in general) is that the analogy of abortion with any of these things is not completely accurate. While we may see some valid points coming from the analogy, there are also a great deal of invalid points made, intentionally or unintentionally from such an analogy.

It occurs to me that we should not throw the baby out with the bathwater, as they say. There is some validity to what Burtchaell and some others are saying about the comparison of abortion and the Holocaust, and by condemning this argument as a whole we are doing them a disservice. There is also a great deal of harm that is done, again intentionally or unintentionally, by espousing this very argument by analogy. The best way I can think of to negotiate this challenge is by abandoning the analogy of abortion and genocide and merely stating the implications of this analogy as serious problems with the practice of abortion. In this sense we remove the sensationalism, the offense that is bound to be felt by Jews, blacks, and other groups, and the

---

[13] Ibid.
[14] Lisa Sowle Cahill, review of *Rachel Weeping*, 252.

rhetoric that incites violence when anti-abortionists are supposed to be ending violence, but we still maintain the important portions of the arguments of Burtchaell and company, that of depersonalization, euphemisms, etc. In other words, if the point cannot be made in any other way than by use of a misleading analogy, it is not much of a point (unless, of course, your only point is to mislead others into believing as you believe).

**Conclusion**
The problem of the analogy of abortion and genocide is not a Pro-Choice problem. It is a Pro-Life problem. Those in the Pro-Life community who wish to express the horrors of abortion, who wish to show that they are hurt by the fact that the unborn are dying at alarming rates, and who support legislation that bans abortion - these are the individuals who are hurt the most by such a misleading argument. Just as I feel responsible to correct those who believe as I believe when they are using offensive, misleading or irrational means of defending the position that we share, there is nobody who is let down more than a Pro-Life individual whose position is ridiculed because of the bad rhetoric of other Pro-Lifers. We have seen the consequences of ends that are achieved by any means necessary throughout the long history of politics, negotiation and war. Achieving a victory by illegitimate means can only lead to negative consequences in the future, perhaps even resulting in the overturning of said victory.

Though I have often been described as iconoclastic, caustically sarcastic, and even disrespectful, I think the proliferation of this analogy is a matter that ought to be handled with care and reverence. I side with individuals who believe that this comparison between abortion and the Holocaust is disrespectful to the families of those who died in the Holocaust as well as the Jewish community (and others) as a whole. I side with the individuals who believe that this comparison between abortion and black slavery is disrespectful to the families of those who suffered through or died as a result of slavery. I also side with those who feel sadness, terror and righteous indignation at the idea of the abortion of a fetus. I would go so far as to say that every human being, Pro-Life or Pro-Choice, should feel for those who have huge gaps in their lives as a result of the death of a fetus, that we should mourn together for those fetuses who are no longer alive as a result of abortion. The reason that we ought to have respect and we ought to mourn is because the human singularity has great value, so much value that no two deaths can ever be compared, let alone the deaths of millions due to the Holocaust and the deaths of millions due to abortion. It is that singularity that Pro-Life supporters intend to do justice to in banning abortion, and that same singularity that Pro-Choice supporters intend to do justice to in taking the decision for abortion out of the hands of legislators. It is because of the human singularity that analogies such as those currently being thrown around cannot stand.

CHAPTER ELEVEN

To Abort or Not to Abort

by Stacey Solomon

**The Law**

Political Science was my undergrad major. I hated it. I only took two classes that made me thankful that I had found my way into this program. One class was Women in Politics and the other was Constitutional Law. In both of these classes we dissected cases including *Roe v. Wade, Planned Parenthood v. Casey, Griswold*, and several others. The individual cases are not exactly fresh in my mind, but the class discussions are. Women have been fighting for equality for centuries. I cannot count how many times I have heard, read, written, and spoken about women's suffrage. The Supreme Court cases dated in the earlier 20<sup>th</sup> century, where women fought for their right to contraception, are examples of women fighting for their equality. My personal view is that the fight for equality stopped with *Roe* and *Doe*. *Roe v. Wade* was not about equality of women, it was about several other things. *Roe* was about the rights of physicians being able to perform abortions without reprimand for doing so. *Roe* was about controlling the population of women living in poverty. *Roe* was about protecting society from illegitimate children. *Roe* had absolutely no undertones of equality for women in it anywhere. Even Justice Rehnquist says: "it is dubious to suggest that women have reached their places in society in reliance upon *Roe* rather than as a result of their determination to obtain higher education and compete with men in the job market, and of society's increasing recognition of their ability to fill positions that were previously thought to be reserved only for men."

In the early part of the 20<sup>th</sup> century, married women fought for the right to freely use birth control. They were afforded the right and later birth control became available to unmarried men and women as well. Several forms of birth control are available now. This allowed for a level of equality for women because women were able to freely participate in sex with their spouse or partner without worrying about continuously getting pregnant. My grandmother died after she had given birth to 13 children. My father was the youngest. She could no longer sustain her own life because of the physical burden that her body was under from so many pregnancies and births. Griswold v. Connecticut helped end tragedies like this by making birth control available so that women could have some level of control over pregnancy. *Roe* allows for women to continuously get pregnant and never give birth to a living baby. *Roe* doesn't allow for free reproductive health choices; *Roe* allows for reproductive cessation. *Roe* gives women a choice, but at a cost.

Feminists disagree with the idea that *Roe* has not given women equality. They claim that women should have the sexual freedom that a man has without the consequence of pregnancy. The problem with that feminist idea is that they claim that sex is a natural act that women should be able to enjoy as much as men do. But pregnancy is the natural consequence to sex. There has to be some kind of compromise. If a woman doesn't want the natural consequence of a natural act to take place in her body then she must take unnatural precautious by using contraception. And although birth control is not one hundred percent fool-proof, abortion shouldn't be the answer. Feminists argue that contraception fails, women are raped and molested, and men take advantage of women. Feminists view abortion as a way to change the course of fate when those things occur; or when a woman just decides that pregnancy is too scary, inconvenient, costly, etc. Extreme feminists even suggest that women shouldn't have to use contraception if they choose not to.

*Planned Parenthood v. Casey* was the first abortion case that the U.S. Supreme Court heard that allowed for provisions to be placed on abortion practices. Pennsylvania had placed several provisions on abortion because abortionists were victimizing women and their "right to choose" and were also greatly benefitting from the profit they made from performing abortions on women. An example of this can be found in Norma McCorvey's book, *Won by Love*, where the abortion doctor would lie to patients about the length of their pregnancy to make extra money. Pennsylvania was not blind to this fact and there was compelling reason for the state to have an interest in protecting their citizens, including the unborn. The provisions placed on abortion forced clinics to inform women of the procedure (informed consent), make them think about their decision and keep clinics from being able to coerce women into an abortion for their profit (24-hour waiting period), force minors to have one parent sign their consent for the abortion unless they get a judicial bypass (parental consent), forcing abortion clinics to report to the government (reporting requirements on abortion facilities), and the requirement for a woman to inform her spouse of an abortion before obtaining one (spousal notification). The only provision that was struck down by the U.S. Supreme Court was spousal notification. This was due to the Court deciding that it may cause further domestic violence and death among women by the hands of their spouses. Also, the Court allowed for the new "undue burden" standard which is defined as a "substantial obstacle in the path of a woman seeking an abortion before the fetus attains viability." The spousal notification provision was the only provision that did not pass the undue burden test. These provisions allowed for the idea of "abortion on demand" to be less attainable, but also finally allowed for some protection of women and their reproductive well-being.

In a way, *Casey* was a victory for the pro-life side. Even though it did nothing to overturn *Roe*, it did allow some legal standards for women and the clinics. Women are not capable of making an appointment and simply showing up to terminate their pregnancy immediately afterward. This means that there is a possibility that at least one woman will change her mind before going through with the procedure because of these provisions. The one provision that is more criticized than the other three that passed was the parental consent provision with judicial bypass. It is the "judicial bypass" part of the provision that is disliked by the pro-life side. A judicial bypass can be too easily obtained by a minor with the help of the clinic and a plausible excuse. Then the parents are still none-the-wiser about their daughter's actions when often young girls do not have the capability to consider their situation rationally and with maturity.

Pro-choicers would claim that any of these provisions are a burden on women. Women should have the free right to choose when she wants, how she wants, and for whatever reasons (or lack thereof) that she decides. However, by allowing women the ultimate freedom to choose, the law also allows for clinics to have the ultimate control over abortion and the ability to treat women however they choose.

As far as the law is concerned, the pro-choice side is clearly winning. Women are free to do as they wish with their unborn children. There have been small victories for the pro-life side, but they are very few and far between.

## Relationship Dynamics

An issue within the abortion debate is the problem of the changing dynamics of the male and female relationship and family dynamics as well. When *Roe* gave women the "right to choose" they actually unbalanced the relationship between men and women in favor of women. There can never be true equality in that case. Sexual practices should be considered equal and respectful and it is true that in the case of accidental pregnancy the woman is the one who has to deal with the issue where the father is free to leave. However, the woman has the right to choose whether or not she wants to allow the child to be born and then she has the choice whether or not to keep the child if it is born. In the case where the woman decides to choose life over abortion and keeping the child rather than putting him or her up for adoption, the father of the child is given no choice in child support. This comes down to the fact that women can choose but men can't. Men can pressure women into abortion or adoption, but they can't force women. In the end, it is her choice, not his. Some say that this is because men try to coerce women into sex in the first place and so many men get women pregnant and abandon them. But if the law makes room for women to be protected in situations like these then why aren't men protected in the case of women intentionally getting pregnant and forcing men into fatherhood? I witnessed an incident such as this more than once.

A woman, I will call her Marie, was in a sexual relationship with a man I will call Jerry. Jerry considers this a casual-sexual relationship with Marie, but Marie wants to be married to Jerry. When Marie and Jerry discuss their feelings about their relationship, Marie believes that the only way Jerry will be serious about their relationship is if she gets pregnant. Marie tells Jerry that she is on the pill, although she is not. Actually, Marie is allergic to birth control pills, but she doesn't tell Jerry. Jerry uses condoms every time they have sex, but Marie purposely compromises them before having sex. Marie becomes pregnant in a short time and cuts communication with Jerry until after the baby is born so that he doesn't pressure her into an abortion. Ten months later, Marie shows up at Jerry's house with their baby in hand. Marie tells Jerry that they should be a family and that she loves him. Jerry is devastated because he had no desire to be a father or a husband. He tells Marie how he honestly feels about the situation. Later, Marie files child support charges against Jerry. Jerry has to pay child support for this child for the next 18 years.

It is no secret that things like this happen to men. The worst part about the issue is that the child is doomed from the moment of conception because it is the child who will suffer the greatest for the actions of his or her parents. The connection with abortion is that giving women the right to choose without giving that right to men allows for the unequal balance and degrades men in the process. Both sides of the abortion debate deny that this behavior is common and some people deny that things like this ever happen. "Unintended" pregnancies are classified as accidental. It is very possible that the man didn't intend to impregnate the woman but the woman intentionally got pregnant. Then the idea that the pregnancy was "unintended" is the only rational way to consider this situation because it's better than blaming the woman for her mental and emotional discord. It is argued back and forth about who is to blame for illegitimate children, and it is often blamed on men.

Women and men will likely never achieve the equality that they desire as long as abortion exists. I believe that a majority of men in the United States are willing and capable of sharing equality with women, but the victimization of men by women and because of abortion is ignored as if it doesn't exist. Partners spend too little time communicating about the possibility of pregnancy when it is a very real occurrence. Couples often don't discuss abortion until a pregnancy arises. Then, the father of the unborn child can get the surprise of his life to find out that his partner is pro-life and has no intentions of aborting their child; or to find out that his partner is going to have an abortion and he is pro-life. The idea that one night stands only occur based on the desires of men is still a commonly accepted idea, and it is false. Women have become exceedingly promiscuous and sexually irresponsible. The tables are turning and women have total control over all of it.

Is it possible that men would be extremely more careful if they knew that they would become a father if their partner got pregnant? If abortion wasn't an option or if they knew that their partner believed that abortion is not the option, would men and women both learn to have better sexual practices? Abortion also allows for both men and women to be careless about their sexual behavior. Too many people consider abortion as a method of birth control. Many men and women have the idea that if they accidentally get pregnant they can get an abortion and not have to worry about birth control beforehand. Some sexually active teens have this view because it's easier to get an abortion than it is to discuss sex with their parents. Some men have this idea because they assume that all women are willing to get an abortion instead of having the child.

**On a Personal Note**
My first personal experience with abortion was in 1993 when I was attending church. The church was rallying for the members to line Abercorn Street from one end to the other (several miles that extends the length of the city) holding signs that read things like "Abortion Kills" and "I am Pro-Life." I was only fourteen years old at the time and really had no concept of abortion at all. My mother and my older sister insisted we go, so we did. I stood out along the south side of Abercorn Street proudly holding my "Abortion Kills" sign and waving at the passing cars for several hours. This is a practice that used to take place once a year (probably on the anniversary of *Roe*) in Savannah, Georgia. It may still continue today. After this experience I decided that I must be pro-life because that is what the church says we should be and that was it. I held strong to the idea, but really gave it little thought. It really had no effect on my life.

I became pregnant at the age of sixteen. I never once thought about abortion, but following a car accident I nearly died from a miscarriage that lasted for over a month before I had a friend take me to the hospital where I was informed about the death of the fetus that I was unaware of carrying. Distraught over the experience, my fiancé and I decided that we would have a child together. My oldest son was born November of the following year. My fiancé had become abusive and I left him, but I never once considered abortion, or adoption. A year later I became pregnant again and miscarried again. The following year my second son was born. I was a mother of two at nineteen years old. I was alone and I was poor. I was happier then with my two boys by my side working my heart out to keep us all fed and sheltered than I have ever been in my life. I gained a sense of integrity and responsibility. I learned that I may have not made the right choices but I would never change them. I eventually married and my husband was unable to have children due to prolonged exposure to Chlamydia. I probably wouldn't know what I was missing if I had aborted my children, but having several miscarriages (two more following my younger son's birth) I can say that it is exceptionally painful to know that my body could not sustain the life that I had conceived. I still live with the inability to accept the fact that my body could not perform its basic function as a woman. I could not possibly imagine the pain and suffering a woman would endure, if not now, eventually, knowing that they terminated the life of their own offspring. They may be ok with the idea now and some women are even proud of what they have done, but I find it unlikely that these women will never feel tormented by their choice.

I have known women who have had abortions who weren't sorry for it. I have known women who gave birth to their children and walked out on them; leaving the child with a family member or even a complete stranger. I went to high school with a girl who hid a pregnancy. She gave birth to a healthy baby boy in her bedroom at her grandparent's house. After the baby was born, she smashed his head in with a golf trophy and left his body in a dumpster. I am a foster parent so I have children living in my home who had mothers that neglected them, beat them, emotionally and mentally abused them and then tossed them to the side. Parents sign over their rights to their children in foster care because it is too inconvenient for them to abide by the demands of the state in order to get their kids back. I have seen what bad parenting does. I live in it every single day of my life. If anyone should be pro-choice, I believe it should be me, but I am not. Babies are innocent whether they were born because of rape, incest, accident, or plain irresponsibility. They were created by an act that is meant for loving, responsible adults and even though the parents may be neither in love nor responsible, that does not give women the right to allow a doctor to rip their unborn child to pieces in order to keep from having to become a parent. There are far too many methods of birth control for abortion to be necessary. Not any of them are fool-proof, but if a person was determined to not have a baby they would use more than one method. There are several birth control methods that can be used simultaneously such as the pill, the sponge, VCF, condoms, and diaphragms. That should do the trick, but even if it doesn't, it should greatly reduce the risk. Also, even though adoption is "the greatest of the three evils," it is an option.[1] Other options are also available. Men and women can participate in reversible sterilization until they desire to have a child. If the government gave grants for tubal ligation or reversible vasectomies, I am sure some people would take up arms against the government for condoning free sexual practices, but our taxes would go further paying for sterilization funding than welfare and food stamps for unwed mothers and their children who are living in poverty. Abortion is a band-aid that the government has used to cover up a plethora of other issues. Society needs to wake up and educate their children on what it means to be a fifteen-year-old parent. Kids are so busy trying to grow up and prove themselves to the world that they destroy their lives before they have a chance to live them. Society allows future generations to carry around too much emotional baggage because we are too occupied with our personal lives to educate our children about life and responsibilities. The impoverished mothers who give birth to unintended babies have to work and allow day cares to raise their children for them. They are supported by minimum wage jobs, tax money, and food stamps. They live in low-income housing and they spend little time teaching their children to have more and do better. Then, the cycle continues and each time there are more children being born and the population of poverty stricken children grows. Abortion has changed none of that. There are still "projects" and ghettos. There are still large families living off of less money in a year than some make in a month. Abortion hasn't fixed any of this. The problem is extreme, but our lawmakers are too worried about being re-elected to make extreme choices to fix extreme issues. People need other options because abortion is brutal and violent. It hurts all persons involved, especially the unborn who suffer the physical torture of being torn apart and ripped from their mother's womb.

I am pro-life because I believe that preventing the problem is better than fixing it after the fact. I am pro-life because I believe

---

[1] See Paul Swope, "Abortion: A Failure to Communicate."

that abortion is brutal and painful. I am pro-life not because I want to see more children live in poverty, but because I believe without the option of abortion people, men and women, would be more responsible for their sexual choices. I am pro-life because abortion has yet to prove to me that it is worthy of its existence.

CHAPTER TWELVE

Against Rebuke and Disgrace

by Marcia Davis-Seale

I survived my TCU graduate class, "The Abortion Debate," and I am changed from it. I find that I am still breathless and blown away, blindsided by the whirlwind of information and insight that gave me a deeper understanding of the tumultuous issues involved, and the emotional and ethical aspects that surround abortion.

I was shocked at how many shades of black and white surfaced with the study on abortion. Likewise, more than two sides–for and against abortion–continues to argue the issue in the public and private arenas, almost four decades after *Roe v. Wade* was decided. I can't begin to cover them all in this column.

I began this class with the idea that "Thou shalt not kill" just about summed it all up; but found that every day the class readings sent me back and forth like a ping pong ball from pro-choice to pro-life, and as often as any, found me at the net.

I was impressed with the defection of abortionist and pro-abortion activist Dr. Bernard Nathanson, who at one time headed the largest abortion clinic in the Western world. He defected from the pro-abortion camp to leadership in the pro-life movement and narrated the graphic "The Silent Scream," anti-abortion film showing in a sonogram the silent scream of a fetus being aborted.

I was stunned by the crossover of Norma McCorvey, the Jane Roe in the *Roe v. Wade* case, to the pro-life side of the issue. McCorvey worked at abortion clinics and went to court for her right to a legal abortion, though the case was decided after the baby in question was born.

She and Nathanson and other abortionists and clinic workers write graphically about the nightmares they had during the time they worked at the clinics: nightmares about the embryonic tissue, the freezer where the aborted tissue was stored in plastic bags, and the tools they used to perform the abortions.

The women who came to the clinics for abortions write about the rebuke, condemnation and aggressive attacks by the "religious" anti-abortion groups protesting along the sidewalks and streets around the clinics. They write about the disgrace and distress they felt.

One comment came out strongly from these women: if they had had just one friend to talk with, to listen to them, that would not judge them or condemn them for their consideration of the abortion option, who would have supported them through the pregnancy and afterwards, they might have been able to step out of the shadow of distress and disgrace and carry their unborn to term. How tragic for all of us to hear that.

Radically real in me grew an awareness of and compassion for the women who were deserted by their men and the unborn children who never had a say; and sadly lacking, I find the wanton society, which hasn't built a solid supportive platform on which women can stand and find shelter under when they find themselves alone and faced with unexpected pregnancy; a society that prefers to invest more energy in arguing the issue than addressing it. And so the argument drones on as lives are lost and futures snuffed out before the first breath. It's about rights: whose rights, what rights? It's about life: whose life (lives), what life (lives)?

I am appalled at the subtle programming of women to discount their own worth, and that of their unplanned unborn, so much so that they hide alone in the silence and the shadows of abortion's tragedy, living out their lives bleeding from the inside from the emotional scars abortion has stamped on them. I was horrified to hear, in the dialogue of one contemporary film on abortion, that women used to paint the corners of their mouths up so they would always appear to be smiling.

I am likewise saddened by the unwanted children who are born, but neglected, abandoned and abused. In contrast, I call to mind a beautiful young couple, that I once had the privilege of calling family, who adopted a beautiful child a few years back. To see the happiness that has flowed out from that adoption for the child, the couple and their extended families vividly colors the other end of the abortion spectrum in my mind's eye.

I believe the shadow of abortion falls on all of us, not just the women who seek or consider them, the men who impregnated them, and the unborn, who never get to be born.

A scripture so often quoted to argue the faith side of the abortion debate include the words from Psalm 139, and I believe it applies here: "For you [Oh, God] created my inmost being; you knit me together in my mother's womb . . . . I am fearfully and wonderfully made . . . . My frame was not hidden from you when I was made in the secret place. When I was woven together in the depths of the earth, your eyes saw my unformed body. All the days ordained for me were written in your book before one of them came to be . . . ."

But I came across another scripture the other day from a daily Bible reading book, quoting Hezekiah in 2 Kings 18:3: "This day is a day of distress and rebuke and disgrace, as when children come to the point of birth and there is no strength to deliver them."

I think we can all do more individually and as a people to build a stronger society that can competently deliver, nurture and love the children waiting to be born as well as the mothers waiting to birth them, and to counter these days of distress and rebuke and disgrace.

## BIBLIOGRAPHY

Arthur, Joyce. "No, Virginia, Abortion Is NOT Genocide." *The Humanist* 60, no. 4 (July/August 2000), 20-23.

Baird, Robert M., and Stuart E. Rosenbaum, eds. *The Ethics of Abortion*, 3rd ed. Amherst, N.Y.: Prometheus Books, 2001.

Baumgardner, Jennifer, ed. *Abortion & Life*. New York: Akashic Books.

Bellinger, Charles. *The Trinitarian Self: The Key to the Puzzle of Violence*. Eugene, Oregon: Pickwick, 2008.

Brown, Robert McAfee. "Abortion and the Holocaust." *Christian Century* 101, no. 33 (October 31, 1984), 1004-1005.

Burtchaell, James T. *Rachel Weeping, and Other Essays on Abortion*. New York: Andrews and McMeel, 1982.

Cahill, Lisa Sowle. Review of *Rachel Weeping*, by James T. Burtchaell. *Journal of Law and Religion* 1, no. 1 (1983): 251-53.

Hamilton, Adam. *Confronting the Controversies: Biblical Perspectives on Tough Issues*. Nashville: Abingdon Press, 2005.

Harris, Lisa H. "Second Trimester Abortion Provision: Breaking the Silence and Changing the Discourse," *Reproductive Health Matters* 16 (2008): 74-81.

Hauerwas, Stanley. "Abortion, Theologically Understood." In *The Hauerwas Reader*, edited by John Berkman and Michael Cartwright, 603-22. Durham, N.C.: Duke University Press, 2001.

Hunt, John. "Abortion and Nazism: Is There Really A Connection?" In *Life and Learning VI: Proceedings of the Sixth University Faculty for Life Conference June 1996 at Georgetown University*, edited by Joseph W. Koterski, 323-36. Washington, D.C.: University Faculty for Life, 1997.

Kaveny, Cathleen. "A Flawed Analogy: Prochoice Politicians & The Third Reich." *Commonweal* 135, no. 12 (June 20, 2008), 6.

McCorvey, Norma L., with Gary Thomas. *Won By Love*. Nashville: Thomas Nelson Publishers, 1997.

McKenna, George. "On Abortion: A Lincolnian Position." *The Atlantic Monthly* 276, no. 3 (September 1995): 51-68.

Mathewes-Green, Frederica. *Real Choices: Listening to Women; Looking for Alternatives to Abortion*. Ben Lomond, Cal.: Conciliar Press, 1997.

Nathanson, Bernard N. *The Hand of God: A Journey from Death to Life by the Abortion Doctor Who Changed His Mind*. Washington, D.C.: Regnery, 1996.

Nathanson, Bernard N., and Richard N. Ostling. *Aborting America*. Garden City, N.Y.: Doubleday, 1979.

Neusner, Jacob. "Israel's Holocaust." *Human Life Review* 25, no. 2 (Spring 1999), 102-03.

Poppema, Suzanne P., with Mike Henderson. *Why I Am An Abortion Doctor*. Amherst, N.Y.: Prometheus Books, 1996.

Schottroff, Luise. *Let the Oppressed Go Free: Feminist Perspectives on the New Testament*. Louisville: John Knox Press, 1993.

Steinem, Gloria. *Outrageous Acts and Everyday Rebellions*. New York: Henry Holt and Company, 1995.

Swope, Paul. "Abortion: A Failure to Communicate." *First Things*, 82 (April, 1998): 31-35.

Tickle, Phyliss, ed. *Confessing Conscience: Churched Women on Abortion*. Nashville: Abingdon Press, 1990.

Ward, Bernadette Waterman. "Abortion as a Sacrament: Mimetic Desire and Sacrifice in Sexual Politics". *Contagion: Journal of Violence, Mimesis, and Culture* 7, no. 1 (2001): 18-35.

West, Traci C. *Disruptive Christian Ethics: When Racism in Women's Lives Matter*. Louisville: Westminster John Knox Press, 2006.

Willis, Ellen. *No More Nice Girls: Countercultural Essays*. Hanover, N.H.: University Press of New England, 1992.

Made in the USA
Lexington, KY
04 April 2014